Junk Drawer

Drawer

ENGINEERING

25 Construction | That Don't
CHALLENGES | Cost a Thing

BOBBY MERCER

CHICAGO
REVIEW
PRESS

Published by Chicago Review Press Incorporated
814 North Franklin Street
Chicago, Illinois 60610
ISBN 978-1-61373-716-3

Library of Congress Cataloging-in-Publication Data
Names: Mercer, Bobby, 1961– author.
Title: Junk drawer engineering : 25 construction challenges that don't cost a
    thing / Bobby Mercer.
Description: Chicago, Illinois : Chicago Review Press Incorporated, [2017] |
    Audience: Ages 9+.
Identifiers: LCCN 2016037089| ISBN 9781613737163 (trade paper : alk. paper) |
    ISBN 9781613737194 (epub) | ISBN 9781613737187 (kindle)
Subjects: LCSH: Engineering—Experiments—Juvenile literature. |
    Science—Experiments—Juvenile literature.
Classification: LCC TA149 .M47 2017 | DDC 620.0078—dc23 LC record available at
https://lccn.loc.gov/2016037089

Cover design: Andrew Brozyna
Interior design: Jonathan Hahn
Photo credits: Bobby Mercer

Printed in the United States of America
5 4 3

**To Jordan and Nicole,
you inspire me daily**

$g = 10 \, m/sec^2$

$E = \frac{1}{2} mv^2$

potential energy

$S = \dfrac{d}{t}$

torque

$W = mg$

$\dfrac{force}{area}$

$F = ma$

pressure $= \dfrac{force}{area}$

$f = \dfrac{1}{T}$

Contents

Acknowledgments

Thanks to all the people who made this book series a reality. The teachers I work with are truly an inspiration to me on a daily basis, and their insight is invaluable. Thanks to Laura Spinks, Jennifer Allsbrook, Sergey Zalevskiy, Kim Mirasola, Leslie Rhinehart, Robert Frost, Lucas Link, and Shannon Haynes. Thanks to the best agent in the business, Kathy Green. Thanks to Jerome Pohlen and the creative people at Chicago Review Press for helping to shape this book. As always, I am eternally grateful to my wife Michele for allowing me and my assistants to make a mess in the name of science. And a special written shout-out to my two personal science assistants, Jordan and Nicole. Their tiny hands are featured in many of the photographs.

$$g = 10 \, m/sec^2 \qquad E = \frac{1}{2}mv^2$$

potential
energy

$$s = \frac{d}{t}$$

torque

$$W = mg$$

$$\frac{force}{area}$$

$$F = ma$$

$$pressure = \frac{force}{area}$$

$$f = \frac{1}{T}$$

Introduction:
What Is Engineering?

Engineering is using science to develop a solution to a problem. *Junk Drawer Engineering* will stimulate brains to think, devise, and build creative solutions. Most of the projects will be challenges that have multiple correct solutions. The key to engineering is trial and error—and learning from the errors.

Good engineering is as much art as it is science. Engineering is seeing a problem and creating a means to fix it. The art of seeing a new way to do something is a skill that gets better with practice. The projects in this book will present you with engineering tasks that let your brain go to work.

Each project will have a suggested material list of low- or no-cost supplies. The material list will be varied, and not all items may be needed. At its core, engineering is trying different things, so feel free to modify the material list based on your creativity and what you have available. Learning to use what you have is the key to *Junk Drawer Engineering*. Complete science kits are fun to do, but creating your own fun from free stuff is even better. It is also good for the environment because you will be able to repurpose stuff you already have. Giving a new life to a broken toy or computer part just makes you feel good.

The instructions may suggest several possible solutions. A basic approach will be shown to give you the ability to do each project, but engineering is about thinking outside the box and devising new ways to do things. You are encouraged to try new methods—you never know what new and creative ways you will think of.

Try new approaches and see what works. Not all approaches will work, but that is OK. Thomas Edison's engineers tried over 2,000 combinations of materials before he found a combination that worked well enough to create the electric light. By the way, Edison did not invent the lightbulb—he just made it better. His greatest contribution to the lightbulb was the screw style socket that is at the bottom of most lightbulbs now. His genius was trying new ideas and never giving up. He knew you can learn a lot from mistakes.

Remember, you will learn for your entire life and along the way you will make some boo-boos. Boo-boos are an opportunity to learn. Any engineering project is only a failure if you don't learn from it. A project is not a failure because it doesn't work right. It is a learning lesson in what needs to be changed. Take a close look at any project and try to figure out what went wrong. Modify the design and try again.

At the end of several of the projects will be photos to show how other people have done these projects. These pictures may be great starting points to modify the project based on an idea you have. Adding your own flair is part of the fun. To me, it has always been most of the fun.

These projects would be perfect for classroom and science camp competitions. Each project will also have a teacher/homeschool parent section on how to adapt the challenges for a variety of levels of intellect and ages. Included are a preschool, elementary school, middle school, and high school adaptation for each project. Since all children are different, it is OK to move up or down the adaptations. A few may only fit one category, but most will be adaptable to many levels.

The key thing is to remember: we learn best when we enjoy what we are doing. Engineering is applying science principles to solve a problem. Science should be fun, so engineering should be fun. Laughter truly is the best medicine and, in my opinion, the best way to learn. If a project fails, laugh about it. A truly spectacular fail will make you laugh. Push the envelope, have fun, and try engineering. Be careful, though—you may learn something along the way.

1

Energy

Energy makes things move. It transports light, sound, and people. The definition of energy is the ability to do work. Engineers deal with how to make energy do what needs to be done. Energy is so much a part of our everyday lives that we often take it for granted. Energy is the unifying concept in all branches of science, and engineering is the use of science to solve problems.

Zip Line Madness

Create a zip line cart—a Zipper—to send an action figure (or golf ball) to the other side of the room.

Engineering Challenge

Engineer a device that will slide down a mini zip line at the greatest speed. The question you need to answer is how to engineer or repurpose something to work as the wheels that roll down the zip line. Zip lines are not just a fun vacation treat, they are a key to learning about science. Speed is the thrill as you zip along. The Zipper needs to slide over the zip line at the top without untying the zip line. You could additionally require a safety line just as all full-size zip line operations do. My contests always included that as a must, because students can easily see the purpose of the extra cable. Engineering is both about design and safety.

In a classroom setting, it might be a good idea to ban store-bought devices that don't have to be modified. Otherwise, a student could buy small pulleys in a home improvement store that would make the wheels part a breeze, making the contest an easy, fast, sure win. They have been forbidden in my contests. If they are allowed, the young engineers should still have to devise a way to suspend the payload from the pulleys. It is a personal choice on whether they are OK to use or not.

Winners can be determined with a stopwatch, as long as the same neutral person is timing every zip. My classes do a March Madness–style tournament with a big bracket sheet on the wall. This entails making two side-by-side zip lines. You can hold both Zippers in place with a ruler and let them go at the same time. You can even have someone use a cell phone to film the finish line for close finishes. Put the teams randomly on the bracket. A bracket eliminates the need for a stopwatch. Students also like picking their team's name. Races add a little fun drama. The winning team gets to take the bracket home as a trophy.

From the Junk Drawer:

- ☐ Sturdy string or nylon cord
- ☐ 2 strong attachment points for the zip line, or 4 for dueling zip lines
- ☐ Paper clips
- ☐ Plastic cup
- ☐ Rubber bands
- ☐ Wheel ideas: modified rubber toy car wheels, small pulleys scavenged from old mini blinds, sewing bobbins, or 2 buttons glued together (don't be afraid to glue things together)
- ☐ Plastic bottle cap
- ☐ Hot glue and glue gun
- ☐ Scissors
- ☐ Hammer and nail
- ☐ Action figure, golf ball, or little stuffed animal. Batman is the most familiar action hero who regularly uses a zip line. In a classroom setting, you might want to use something that is gender neutral. Women make up a very large part of engineering majors now.
- ☐ For zip line race bracket: Poster board and marker, and cell phone (to film really close finishes)
- ☐ Sturdy tape (optional)

Step 1: Tie one end of the zip line cord to a sturdy base. The top needs to be high. You can use the top of a cabinet, the top hinge of a door, or the back of a chair (depending on the age of children). You can also use tape to secure this end if it is sturdy tape.

Step 2: Attach the other end of the zip line to a lower point on the other side of the room. The line needs to be pulled tight and not have any visible sag. A great idea is to tie the bottom to a chair or desk. You can move the chair to pull the zip line taut.

Step 3: Unfold a paper clip.

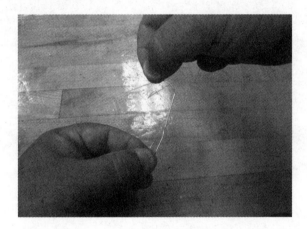

Step 4: Build a harness for the zip line rider. You can do this with string, thin wire, and rubber bands, or you can use a plastic cup to create a gondola that hangs from your trolley. Steps 5 through 8 will show you how to make a gondola for your toy.

Step 5: Wrap a rubber band around the top of a plastic cup.

Step 6: Find two identical rubber bands for the next two steps. Slide one rubber band underneath the rubber band wrapped around the cup, as shown.

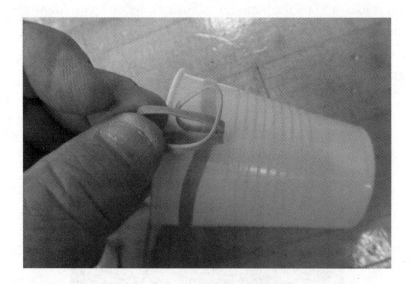

Step 7: Slide one loop of this rubber band through the other loop and pull tight. Repeat for the other side of the cup.

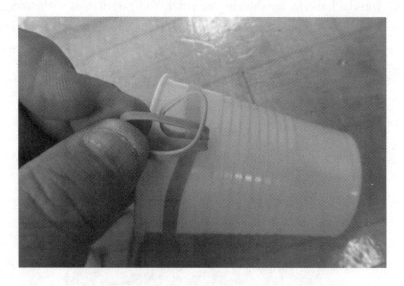

Step 8: Pick up the cup by the two rubber bands. You might have to move the rubber bands slightly to get it to hang correctly. Put the toy rider in the cup (your Zipper) and you are ready to zip.

Step 9: Slide the unfolded paper clip through the loop at the top of your toy (or gondola). Side the other end of your paper clip over the tallest point of your zip line. Let it go and watch it zip. Building a wheel that rolls will make your design faster.

Step 10: Devise some type of pulley wheel to go over the zip line. You want something that will roll freely and stay on the line. Sewing bobbins, pulleys out of old mini blinds, and modified car toy wheels can all work.

Here is how to make one out of a bottle cap and hot glue gun. *This method should only be done with adult supervision.* (If you have a suitable wheel, skip to step 13.) Put a line of hot glue around one edge of a plastic bottle cap. Be careful since the glue is very hot and can burn. Let it cool for at least two minutes before you do step 11.

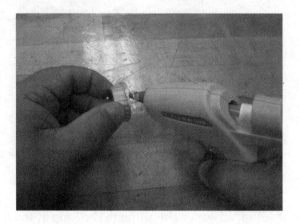

Step 11: Repeat on the other side. After it cools, you can use scissors to trim it so it looks good.

Step 12: Use a small nail and a hammer to create a hole in the center of your bottle cap.

Step 13: Attach the toy (or gondola) to the wheeled trolley you made by hooking the paper clip through the hole in the bottle cap.

Step 14: Slide the wheel over the top of the zip line. This is easy, since one side of the paper clip is open. Let it go and watch it zip.

For a Zip Line Madness Tournament

Step 15: Load a second zip line device on the other line if you are doing a bracket challenge. Have the team members hold their zip line devices at the top.

Step 16: Position one team member at the bottom to catch the zip line devices as they finish. Make sure you have agreed on a finish line before you let the Zippers go. If you have limited help, you might want to put a pillow at the end to act as a finish line. The pillow will help keep the Zipper in good shape for another contest.

Position a person with a cell phone at the finish line. The phone must be perpendicular to the zip lines. A selfie stick is great tool to hold the finish line camera. Start the camera, then have a countdown and let them go. Only consult the phone camera if it is not obvious who the winner is.

The Science Behind It

Zip lines are all about potential energy, kinetic energy, and friction. At the top of the zip line, the trolley and the load are entirely gravitational potential energy. Gravitational potential energy (GPE) is the stored energy in an object because of its mass and height above the ground. As they zip down the line, the GPE is converted into kinetic energy. Kinetic energy (KE) is related to mass and speed. Some GPE is "lost" to heat by the friction of the wheels and the zip line rubbing together. The "lost" energy is actually just heat being created.

The best Zipper is the one with the least friction. Less friction means more GPE goes into KE than heat, and more KE means more speed. Creating low-friction wheels is important in bicycles, cars, and any design that involves rolling.

Zip lines also have safety lines that attach to the overhead cables in addition to the trolley you are riding on. The safety line is a great reminder that with great engineering knowledge comes great responsibility. Safety in all engineering challenges is important. The next time you go on any ride on vacation, look for the safety that is engineered into the ride.

Age-Appropriate Engineering

This is a fun activity for all four age groups—preschool, elementary, middle school, and high school. With preschoolers, the experience of making their own Zippers is enough. No stopwatches or brackets are needed at that age—just suspending the Zipper from paper clips hooked to the line will yield success. For early elementary students, contests may be fun, but unnecessary. That depends on how basketball crazy your area is. The March Madness fever that annually takes over large parts of the country plays naturally to this contest. It also sends students home with a natural bridge into adult conversation when the subject of March Madness comes up.

For middle schoolers, you can add in the math. Have the students calculate average speed (distance/time) and compare GPE and KE. The contest idea may also be fun and a natural parent-child conversation starter.

In high school, this activity can reach almost college level when you add in all math aspects. You can calculate everything mentioned previously plus more. Since you started at rest, the final speed is twice your initial speed. This allows you to calculate a very accurate final KE. Calculate the initial GPE, subtract the final KE, and you have the work done by friction. The initial GPE is found with the equation GPE = mgh, where m is the mass in kilograms, g is 9.8 meters per second squared, and h is the height in meters. Your GPE units will be a N-m (Newton meter), also called a joule. The final KE is found by KE = ½ m(v squared), where v is velocity. The KE unit is also a N-m. When you subtract the initial GPE from the final KE, you will have the energy "lost" due to friction, or to heat. Since work = Fd, if you divide work done by friction ("lost" energy) the length of the zip line in meters, you will have the average force of friction (in Newtons) during the ride. This allows you to calculate the average force of friction. The math possibilities are endless.

Zip Line Madness is a fun engineering activity for all ages. Fashion a Zipper and have some fun, whether going solo or racing.

Lunchroom Catapult

Launch marshmallows across the room with a catapult.

Engineering Challenge

Design and build a catapult using common materials available in most cafeterias. The challenge can easily be modified for a variety of age groups. The material list is also easy to modify based on what you have available. The winner is the catapult that sends the marshmallow the farthest. Ping-Pong balls, balled up paper, or small bouncy balls can be substituted for the marshmallows. Launching rule modifications will be covered in the Age-Appropriate Engineering section.

The list here includes what I use in my classroom, but it can vary based on what is on hand. The only essential requirement is a plastic spoon to act as the launcher.

From the Junk Drawer:

- ☐ 15 craft sticks
- ☐ 15 rubber bands
- ☐ Plastic spoon (cheap spoons work better because they bend more)
- ☐ Mini marshmallows or other small, launchable objects
- ☐ Hot glue, hot glue gun, and tape (optional)

The following are ways to do the challenge that work well using just the materials above. As with all *Junk Drawer Engineering* projects, feel free to modify and adapt based on what you have and try new ideas.

Step 1: Stack five or six craft sticks together. Wrap a rubber band around each end. Keep wrapping the rubber bands until they are very tight.

Step 2: Place another craft stick underneath the sticks you just banded together. Wrap a rubber band around the point where they cross using a crisscross style so that it is securely held in place.

Step 3: Place a craft stick halfway under the spoon handle and wrap two rubber bands around it to extend the handle.

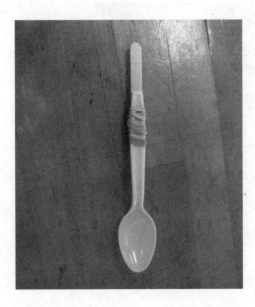

Step 4: Place the long-handled spoon on top of the cross you made earlier. You want about 1 inch of overlap beyond the bottom craft stick. You may need to adjust the craft stick on the bottom.

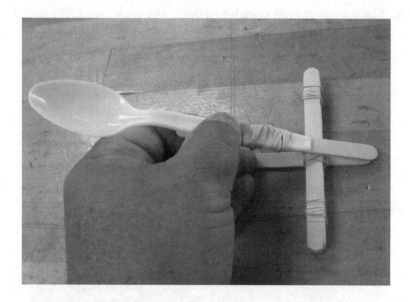

Step 5: Pick up the catapult and twist a very strong rubber band around the *V* created by the long spoon handle and the bottom craft stick. Keep twisting the band until it is very tight.

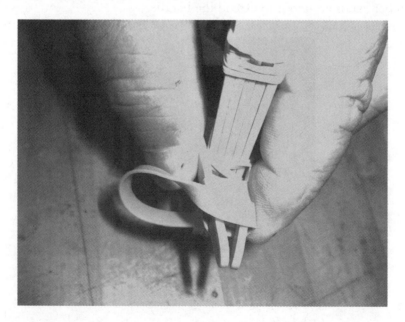

Step 6: To use your catapult, load your mini marshmallow or other ammo into the spoon. Use a finger to pull back the top of the spoon, and then let it go. You might want to use your other hand to hold the base to get a longer, steadier pull.

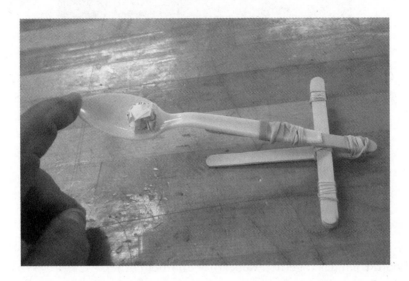

Step 7: Here is another style you can build out of the same materials listed previously. Cross two craft sticks so they make a long *V* shape and wrap a rubber band around where they cross. Keep looping it over the ends and make it very tight.

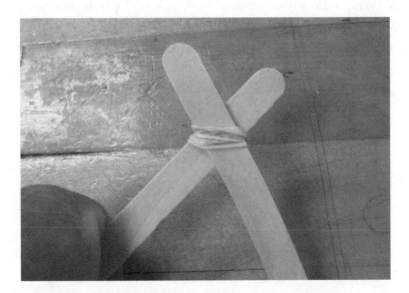

Step 8: Repeat for two more corners so you create a craft stick triangle, as shown. Repeat steps 7 and 8 to make two craft stick triangles. Adjust the corners until the two triangles are approximately the same size.

Step 9: Stack the two triangles up and use a rubber band to secure one corner of both triangles together. Repeat for another corner.

Step 10: Slide a craft stick between the two triangles and stand it up on edge. The two triangles should take on the shape of an alligator's mouth.

Step 11: Wrap rubber bands around both ends of the craft stick you just put in. Make sure the craft stick stays upright to keep the correct shape. Wrap the rubber bands around until the assembly is tightly held together.

Step 12: Set the alligator mouth down. Stand a craft stick up in the open end of the alligator's mouth. Wrap the two points where it sits in the *V* of the triangles. You want to keep the craft stick turned at the orientation shown here. This is easiest once both rubber bands are on. Twist it until it looks like the picture below.

Step 13: Slide the bottom of the spoon under one or two loops of the top rubber band to hold the spoon upright.

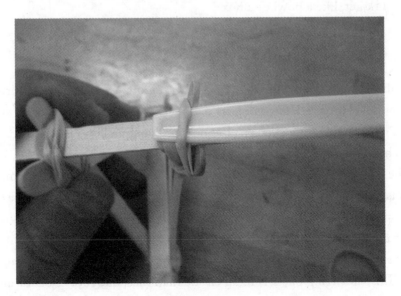

Step 14: Wrap another rubber band higher on the spoon to secure it to the craft stick that is standing up.

Step 15: Your finished catapult is ready to load and fire. Place the ammo in the bowl of the spoon, pull it back with your finger, and let it go. You probably want to place your other hand firmly on the catapult base to get the strongest pull. How could you modify your catapult to make it throw your ammo farther?

Step 16: Shoot your ammo for distance. Another fun challenge is to shoot for a target, like a bowl or a box.

The Science Behind It

Catapults use energy to launch projectiles. Catapults were one of the earliest weapons developed to launch objects over long distances. Catapults are fun and entertaining engineering projects. Launching marshmallows is safe, and you always have leftovers to eat.

The energy comes primarily from the flexibility of the throwing arm. The spoon is flexible. When you secure the spoon at one end and pull on the tip of the spoon, you are adding elastic potential energy (EPE) to the spoon. The greater the bend, the greater the elastic potential energy. The spoon wants to stay straight, so when you let go it will spring back to its original straight shape. This "springing back" is in all elastic materials, like rubber bands and the elastic in the top of your socks. Potential means stored, so when you bend the spoon, you are storing elastic potential energy in the spoon. When you release the spoon, this elastic energy is turned into the energy of motion of the marshmallow. Energy of motion is called kinetic energy by engineers.

You also can create more elastic potential energy by using rubber bands. Stretching the rubber bands adds additional elastic potential energy. Putting more elastic potential energy in means more kinetic energy for the marshmallow going out—the marshmallow goes farther.

Creating a longer lever arm will help you engineer a better catapult. Catapults use torque. Torque is a force that causes objects to rotate. Torque is the force applied multiplied by the length of the lever arm. An easy way to understand this is with a door. It takes a certain amount of torque to open any door. If you push on the door handle it takes very little force, since the door handle is a large distance away from the hinge. But when you push close to the hinge, you have to push much harder because the lever arm is shorter. A longer lever arm on your catapult will allow you to create more torque on the spoon. More torque will add to your distance.

The other engineering challenge with catapults is stability to handle the torque. As you apply a torque to the spoon, it is going to try to rotate your entire catapult. Your catapult needs to be able to handle that torque. If you are allowed to use two hands, you can hold the base with one hand to add stability. But if you are only allowed one hand, you need a large enough base to keep the base flat as you apply a force to your spoon.

Age-Appropriate Engineering

The Lunchroom Catapult is a great engineering project for all ages. Even toddlers can learn the principles by holding a spoon at one end and launching marshmallows by pulling on the tip of the spoon and letting go. This engineering skill may be a bad idea when the toddler gets bored at dinnertime.

For early elementary age, catapults with rubber bands and craft sticks are the way to go. Younger engineers should be allowed to use two hands to launch their Lunchroom Catapult. Also, you could let the students tape the base safely down to a tabletop to help with stability. You also might need to help teach kids this age how to wrap rubber bands around a joint multiple times to hold it tight.

With upper elementary and middle school students, hot glue could be allowed if students are mature enough. Err on the side of safety if in doubt. Using two hands to launch for these ages may be appropriate. For this age, you can also add the science of projectiles and launch angles if desired. A good idea for this age and older is to stress that the catapult must be portable, so it can't be taped to the tabletop.

For high school age students, hot glue is OK with a few safety reminders. But my high school students actually do the project with just rubber bands, craft sticks, and spoons. Your art teacher probably has hot glue guns you can borrow, though they can be found quite cheaply. A challenging modification you can make for high school students is to require that they only use one finger to launch the Lunchroom Catapult. This stresses that the catapult needs to be able to handle the torque required. Depending on the academic level of the students, add math. In a physics class, you can have the students calculate the launch angle and speed by measuring time in the air and horizontal distance. Launching marshmallows is a fun way to study projectiles. You can also try launching different types of objects to talk about the aerodynamics of your projectiles.

With all levels, what you launch is completely up to what you have on hand. Small foods like marshmallows and grapes are fun, but small rubber balls and balled up pieces of paper work just as well.

Bounce with Me

Design a bungee cord ride for your favorite toy.

Engineering Challenge

Design your own bungee cord using rubber bands. The goal is to get your toy the closest to the floor as it bounces up and down on the cord. A cell phone video camera is a great way to see who the winners are. The supplies can have a fixed number of rubber bands or an unlimited number. The choice is up to the judge and the number of rubber bands on hand.

Another goal could be to come within a certain distance of the ground without hitting the ground. Six inches is a reasonable distance for most students. An additional challenge for older students can be to attach the rubber bands to the cup without using tape or cutting the rubber bands.

From the Junk Drawer:

- ☐ Plastic or foam cup (any size); this is a great use for used cups after snack time or lunch as long as they are rinsed out and dried
- ☐ Something to act as a weight (that will fit inside your cup)
- ☐ Rubber bands (any size)
- ☐ Table edge from which your design will hang
- ☐ Tape (or extra sets of hands)
- ☐ Action figure or small toy (not required but fun)

Step 1: Place a weight inside your cup. A baseball is used here, but it can be almost anything.

Step 2: Put a rubber band around the cup beneath the lip of the cup, as shown.

Step 3: Select two rubber bands that are the same size. Slide one of the two rubber bands underneath the rubber band already on the cup.

Step 4: Take one end of the rubber band and slide it through the loop on the other side of the cup rubber band. Pull it tight enough to hold it in place, but not super tight. Repeat steps 3 and 4 for the other side.

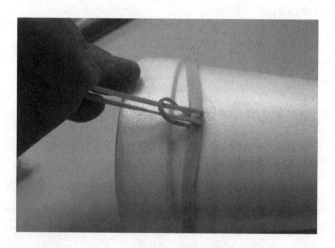

Step 5: Pick the cup up with the top loops of both of these rubber bands. Move the rubber bands around the cup until the cup hangs perfectly straight.

Step 6: Slide a rubber band through the top two loops and hold it in place.

Step 7: Slide one end through the other end's loop. Hang the cup from the top of this band to pull it tight.

Step 8: Slide another rubber band through the top of the rubber band from step 7.

Step 9: Slide one end through the other end's loop.

Step 10: Pull it tight again by hanging the cup freely at the end of the rubber band bungee cord.

Step 11: Now is a good time to test the length. With one hand, hold the top of the rubber band bungee at the table height. If it hangs more than halfway to the floor, you will have to remove some rubber bands. A good starting point is about one-third of the way from the table to the floor when the Bounce with Me bungee cord is hanging still. You can add more bands if needed.

Step 12: Once your bungee cord is the right length, it is time for your first trial run! Add your toy to the cup. The toy is optional, but it is a fun option enjoyed by children of all ages. Hold the cup at table level with one hand and the end of your bungee on the table with the other hand. Let the cup go, but hold on to the end of the bungee cord. You can use tape to hold the end of the bungee cord to the table as shown.

Step 13: For a contest, tape a ruler or meter stick behind the bungee cord. You can have someone eyeball the height or use a cell phone to record it. With most cell phones, you can play it back in slow motion to get the exact height. The cell phone and the person eyeballing the height need to be at ground level. A cell phone could be held in place with a selfie stick or cell phone tripod. How close to the floor was it? Add another rubber band if you want to try to get closer without hitting the floor.

The Science Behind It

Bungee cords convert gravitational potential energy (GPE) into elastic potential energy (EPE). At the top of your bungee cord, the weight and toy contain only GPE. At the lowest bounce, the weight and toy only contain EPE. In the middle of bounces, you can have GPE, EPE, and kinetic energy (KE). Those three forms of energy are collectively called mechanical energy. The bungee cords simply help the three types trade back and forth.

Total energy must be conserved . . . it's the law: the law of conservation of energy. That means the *amount* of energy stays the same. But it can change form: some of the mechanical energy is converted into thermal energy on each bounce—the rubber bands actually heat up. You can prove this to yourself using a new rubber band. Hold an unstretched new rubber band against your bottom lip. Then stretch it very fast and immediately touch it back to your bottom lip. It will be warmer. Since some mechanical energy is converted into thermal energy—heat—each bounce will be a little smaller. Total energy includes thermal energy and is conserved. But mechanical energy actually decreases with each bounce.

Bungee cord jump amusement rides have several different bungees for people of different sizes. Gravitational potential energy depends upon how big you are. Bigger people need a stronger bungee to avoid the ground. The bungee is a spring and springs are different. Every spring has its own spring constant. The spring constant tells you how much a spring is going to stretch when a certain force is applied. As an added safety feature, most bungee rides are done over safety pads or water. Hitting a pad or water is safer than hitting a hard surface.

Age-Appropriate Engineering

This is a fun engineering activity for all ages. Let the students use a favorite toy. Even high school students enjoy digging through their old toys for a favorite to repurpose.

Middle and high school students can handle the math, so the equations for each can be used. Advanced high school students can even calculate the spring constant for each bungee. If you have one, you can even set a motion detector up under the weight/toy combination and create a graph of the motion. Cell phone video recorders can also let you examine each bounce to see how much mechanical energy is lost each bounce.

Gravity Slide

Engineer the fastest slide on the planet, or the slowest.

Engineering Challenge

Choose materials that give you the fastest slide down a ramp. Keep the weight of your slider the same in each case so that the surfaces are being tested, not the weight. Friction depends upon the normal force (the weight of the slider pushing down) and the two surfaces in contact. Let the students figure out on their own that you have two surface materials that can be varied. Give them a hint at some point if they are not realizing that, but usually somebody figures it out before you can tell them. You want them to create the fastest slide. Test the materials first and then build the slide and let it ride.

For a great extension, have them decide on materials for a slide that is the slowest. If you have enough of the surface materials, let them build it.

From the Junk Drawer:

☐ Shoe box (or any small container)
☐ Weight to add to box (could be a shoe)
☐ Piece of board to act as a ramp
☐ Protractor
☐ Tape

☐ Wax paper
☐ Aluminum foil
☐ Paper
☐ 2 mouse pads
☐ Other materials (sandpaper, wrapping paper, etc.)

In a classroom setting, you could do this experiment in one day or two. For two, build just the ramp and box on the first day to get a gut feeling for friction and let students think of other low (or high) friction surfaces at home. Let them bring in materials the next day and test them out.

Step 1: Add weight to the shoe box. Place the shoe box on the board.

Step 2: Slowly increase the angle of the board until the shoe box just barely begins to slide down the ramp. Repeat it if you are unsure. The box should always start sliding at about the same angle.

Step 3: Look at your protractor carefully. The horizontal lines that represent 0 and 180 degrees are not on the bottom of most protractors. You need to locate the small hole or cross that is at the center of that line. The angle you are measuring must go through this point.

Step 4: It is easiest to measure the bottom of the ramp for the angle. Put the protractor flat on the table. Slide it until the point you found in the previous step is lined up with the bottom of the ramp, as shown. You must move your eye down to that level to read the protractor. The angle is where the **bottom** of the ramp crosses the angle readings on the protractor.

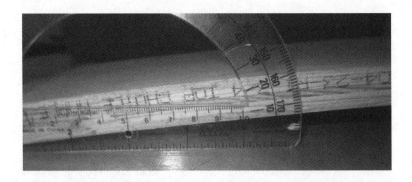

Step 5: Tape a new surface material to the bottom of the shoe box. The tape must only be on the side of the box, not underneath. Wax paper is shown in the picture, which is very smooth.

Step 6: Repeat steps 1 through 4 and read the angle from the protractor.

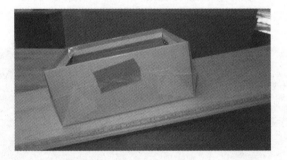

Step 7: Try all the different surfaces to find the one with the least friction. The surface with the least friction is the one that allows the box to slide when tilted at the smallest angle. What do you notice about that surface? Slide your hand across it—what do you feel?

Step 8: Once you have found the surface with lowest friction, put that surface also on the ramp. Again, be careful to only tape the sides and bottom of the ramp. Tape between the two surfaces would affect the slider. Now tilt the ramp until the box starts to slide. Is the angle bigger or smaller now? You have now created the fastest Gravity Slide.

Step 9: For fun, now create the *slowest* slide ever. Which surface from earlier tests had the most friction? Put that surface on the bottom of the shoe box. Remember, you only want tape on the sides or top of the box.

Put the same surface on your ramp, even if you only have a small piece. This will still show you terrific amounts of friction even though you probably can't cover the entire slide. Slowly increase the ramp until the box begins to slide. You have now created the world's slowest Gravity Slide. At least it is the slowest Gravity Slide you have ever made. Shown here are two mousepads with the black rubber sides together. Can you find a surface that has more friction?

Step 10: This is also the same process you would use to test which shoes are best for basketball, tennis, and volleyball. For those sports, you want a lot of friction, so that your shoes won't slide. Test a few of your different shoes by placing them on the ramp and increasing the angle until they start to slide. The highest angle is the best volleyball shoe. The lowest angle would be the best shoe for dancing or bowling, where you might want to slide a little.

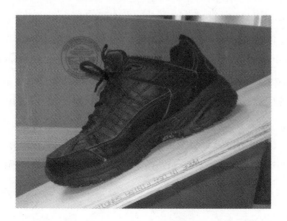

The Science Behind It

At the top of a slide, an object has gravitational potential energy (GPE). As the object slides down, the GPE is turned into kinetic energy. But friction is going to work against this conversion. Friction creates heat and lowers the sliding object's final speed (and kinetic energy). More friction means less speed.

Slides want to minimize friction. They do this by being super smooth. Smoother surfaces have fewer microscopic bumps and are easier to slide on.

Friction also depends upon the normal force, which is a tougher concept. Isaac Newton's third law of motion states that for every action there is an equal and opposite reaction. If you push on a wall, the wall pushes back with the exact same amount of force, but in the opposite direction. Your weight pulls you down, but the floor pushes back with a force that is equal and opposite in direction. This reaction force coming out of the floor is called the normal force because it is perpendicular to the floor.

Slides are a little more complicated. When you sit on a slide at an angle, your weight goes straight down toward the center of Earth. But there are two parts to the weight on a ramp.

Part of the weight pulls you down the ramp and part of the weight pulls you into the ramp. The part that pulls you into the ramp is balanced by the perpendicular force (normal force) that acts out of the ramp. In other words, the ramp pushes back with normal force that is equal and opposite to the part of weight that acts into the ramp. As you make a ramp steeper, the part of the weight going into the ramp gets smaller, so the normal force gets smaller.

The second part is the part of weight that goes down the face of the ramp. When you are on a flat surface like a floor, the part going down the ramp is zero because the angle of the floor is zero. Your weight is equal to the normal force. As the ramp angle increases, the part going down the face of the ramp gets bigger. If the ramp is perfectly upright, all of the weight acts down the ramp and there is no normal force, because none of the weight pushes into the ramp.

If you put both of these together, as you increase the angle of a ramp, the part of weight going down the ramp increases and the part going into the ramp decreases. When the force going down is greater than the force of the friction holding it in place, the box will begin to do the Gravity Slide.

Since the frictional force depends upon the two surfaces in contact, we get faster slides with two super smooth materials. And you want the steepest slide that is safe. Your shoe box can be tested at extreme speeds, but in real life applications, that might hurt people. So playground slides usually have a super-smooth surface at a medium angle—steeper for the older children and not so steep for the little ones. The clothes you wear can also affect your speed. Wear silky clothing and you will slide faster than if you are wearing blue jeans.

In a playground you never see a slide with a rubber or sandpaper surface. It would have way too much friction, and even if you did slide, it would hurt. You will see rubber "slides" on conveyor belts in large factories because these belts use increased friction to keep the objects in place while they move around the factory. As they manufacture objects, they want them to ride the conveyor belt and not slide back down.

Age-Appropriate Engineering

For the youngest students, measuring the angles might be beyond their level. But seeing that different materials are easier to slide on is a great learning point. Friction is a concept that children at that age can grasp. They use playground slides, so they can understand the concept of the smooth surface being good for slides.

For upper elementary and middle school students, teaching them how to use a protractor is great, or if they already know, a great review. Friction is around them all the time. They know they have a pair of shoes for playing sports and a pair of shoes to wear to weddings and church. The shoes have different surfaces and have different friction.

For high school students, they can understand everything related to friction. For advanced level students, they can even do the math. The complete math involves sine and cosine, so they must know those concepts for this level.

For almost all levels, they can measure distance down the ramp and time with a stopwatch to calculate the average speed of their Gravity Slide.

Marbleous Roller Coaster

Create a fun roller coaster as you learn its secrets.

Engineering Challenge

Create a basic marble roller coaster from recyclable materials to learn the basics of roller coaster design. The goal is to go from top to bottom without a spill. If you have a spill, you've just learned what doesn't work. Adjust your track and try again.

From the Junk Drawer:

- ☐ Empty paper towel and toilet paper tubes
- ☐ Empty cereal boxes, pasta boxes, etc.
- ☐ Plastic drink bottles, foam cups, etc.
- ☐ Plastic cup for target
- ☐ Scissors
- ☐ Painter's tape
- ☐ Foam core, large piece of cardboard, or a wall
- ☐ Marbles or small rubber balls

Step 1: Using scissors, cut all of the empty tubes lengthwise. Try to make the cuts as straight as possible.

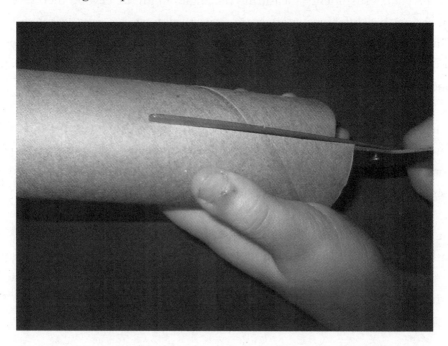

Step 2: Repeat the cut for the other side so that you are left with two half tubes from each tube. These will form the bulk of your track pieces unless you try some of the other options.

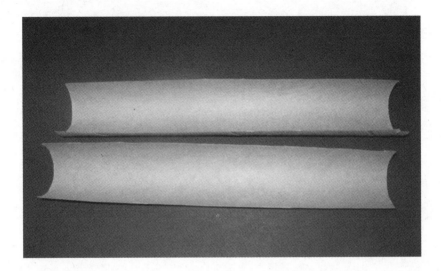

Step 3: Use painter's tape to secure the top of the track to your work surface. The surface can be a piece of foam core, a large piece of cardboard or white board, the side of a refrigerator, or even a wall—any large, flat surface that can be made vertical. Painter's tape works best because it will come off easily without removing paint. It also can be removed and re-stuck easier than most other kinds of tape.

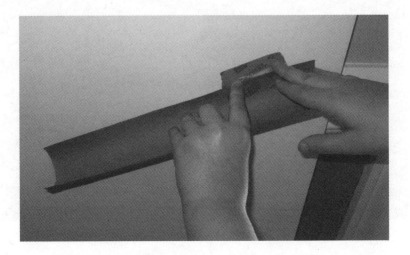

Step 4: Use another piece of tape to secure the other end of the track.

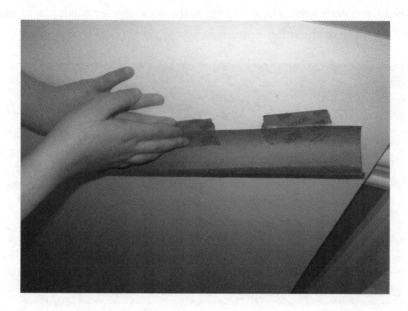

Step 5: Put another track below the first. You can guess where the marble is going to roll, but you will test it in the next step anyway.

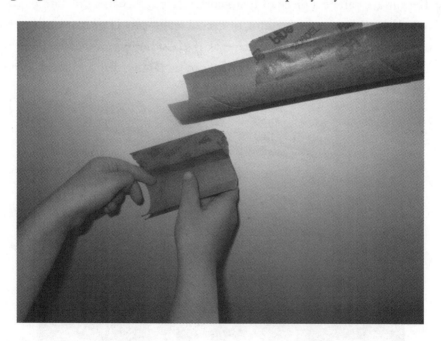

Step 6: Gently place the marble at the top of your track with one hand. Use the other hand to try to catch the marble as it leaves the second track. If the marble misses the second track, move the track and try again. The painter's tape makes it easy to reposition the track.

Step 7: For a cool option, you can add foam or leftover fast food cups. Cut a marble-sized hole in the bottom of a foam cup. The hole needs to be near the side so the marble can be close to the vertical surface to fall where it will hit the next track.

Step 8: Add the cup at the end of one of the tracks. Use one or two pieces of tape to secure the top of the cup.

Step 9: Use a very long piece of tape to secure the bottom of the cup to the surface.

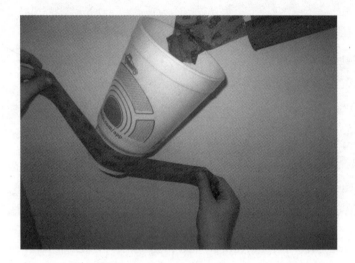

Step 10: Cereal boxes are also a great material for creating marble tracks. Cut about 1 inch up from the narrow side of the box, as shown. You are going to use the narrow sides as the track to roll the marbles down.

Step 11: When you get to the bottom of the box, simply keep cutting right around the bottom. Negotiating around the corner is tough, but with practice you can do it.

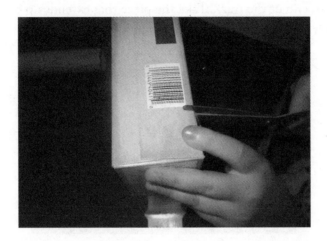

Step 12: Finish cutting up the other side. You will be left with a rectangular track with two sides, one closed end, and one open end.

Step 13: Place this track beneath the last track (or cup). Make sure the closed end is on the high side—otherwise, your marble will stop. Remember to test your tracks from the top after you add any new piece of track.

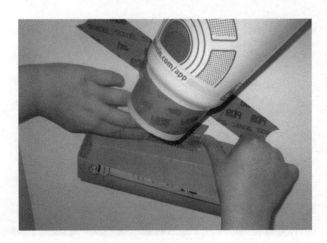

Step 14: Continue adding tracks and testing your design after each part is added. Move each track as you go if needed to keep the marble rolling.

Step 15: If your marble goes off the high end of a track, you can add an end to block it. Use a piece of tape—about 6 inches is good. Attach about 2 inches to the bottom of the track and wrap 4 inches straight up along the open, high end of the track. Take the piece that extends up over the end and fold it down on itself to cover up the sticky part.

Step 16: You may need to add a sideways piece of tape to this end to keep it in place.

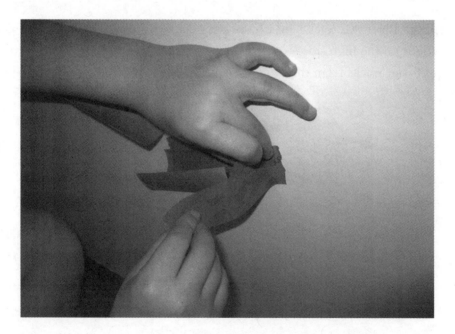

Step 17: Keep adding tracks until you reach the finish cup. Always remember to test after you add each piece as you guide the marble to the final cup.

Step 18: Stand back and take a look at your creation. Send a marble down and enjoy your Marbleous Roller Coaster. Show it off to your friends and family.

The Science Behind It

Almost all roller coasters are all about converting gravitational potential energy into kinetic energy. Gravitational potential energy is related to the weight (mass times the acceleration of gravity) of the object and the height. Kinetic energy is related to the mass of the object and the speed.

Almost all roller coasters start with a lift hill. The lift hill has a motor connected to a chain like a bike chain. This chain pulls the roller coaster car to the top of the hill so that it has lots of gravitational potential energy. The car then rolls freely down the track, converting gravitational potential energy into kinetic energy.

Age-Appropriate Engineering

This really is an engineering activity for all ages. For advanced students, they could jump straight to the Leap of Faith roller coaster (page **46**) which involves the same concepts.

Slow Down

Create the world's slowest roller coaster.

Engineering Challenge

Here's an interesting challenge. Each team starts building a marble track at the same height. The team that takes the *most* time to reach the target at the bottom will be the winner. The only rule is that the marble must roll on its own all the way to the ground—no help if it gets stuck. If it gets stuck, you go back to the engineering drawing board and try again. Just remember, slow and steady wins the race, or at least this race.

From the Junk Drawer:

☐ Paper towel tubes
☐ Toilet paper tubes
☐ Empty cereal boxes, pasta boxes, etc.
☐ Plastic drink bottles, foam cups, etc. (optional)
☐ Scissors
☐ Painter's tape

☐ Foam core, large piece of cardboard, or a wall

☐ Plastic cup for target

☐ Marble or small rubber ball

☐ Paper and pencil for planning

☐ Stopwatch

Step 1: Cut the paper towel and toilet paper tubes lengthwise with scissors. (For reference photo, see page 32.)

Step 2: Do the same along the opposite length. You will be left with two tracks from each tube you cut. (For reference photo, see page 33.)

Step 3: Find a flat surface to build this roller coaster on. You can use a wall, a whiteboard, a large piece of cardboard, or foam core. Label a starting point.

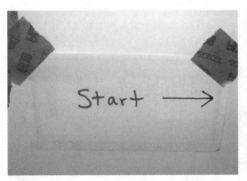

Step 4: Label a finish point and put a target cup down to catch the marble. For a contest, all groups should have the same starting height and finish height.

Step 5: Secure the top of your track with a small piece of painter's tape. This tape is the best choice because it is easy to reposition without leaving a mark on your surface or taking paint off a wall. Use one hand to hold the bottom of the track as you go to the next step.

Step 6: Test running the marble down the track. You want it to roll as slowly as possible, but you don't want it to stop. Catch the marble at the bottom. Adjust the angle of the track until you find the point at which the marble rolls the slowest. Add tape at the bottom end of the track to hold it in place.

Step 7: Add another track or two. When you get ready to change directions, you will need to place the next track under the end of the previous one and angle it downward the opposite way.

Step 8: Keep adding more tracks, testing it after each track is added. It is a good idea to start from the top each time.

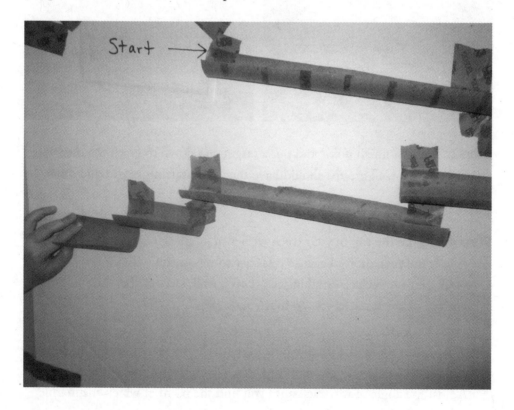

Step 9: You may want to tape a leftover piece of cardboard to the end of a track for the marble to bounce off to keep it in the track. Remember, slow wins, so rolling up and hitting the end when the marble changes directions will help it take more time to reach the bottom.

Step 10: Keep adding more tracks and testing each time. Reposition the tracks as needed. Painter's tape makes that easier than most other kinds of tape.

Step 11: Keep going! The more tracks, the longer it should take the marble to reach the bottom.

Step 12: Remember, you are trying to reach the finish cup. If the rules allow it, or you are not in a contest, you can move the cup as long as you keep it at the same height.

Step 13: Stand back and let it roll. Move any tracks if you need to, or add ends to the directional change tracks if the ball goes off the track. You can also add tape to the front of any tracks to keep the ball from rolling off the front.

Step 14: A fun option is to just keep dropping marbles onto the track. See how many you can get rolling at the same time. Show off the world's slowest roller coaster to family and friends. A foam- or cardboard-backed Slow Down roller coaster can go home with one team member.

The Science Behind It

Almost all roller coasters are all about converting gravitational potential energy (GPE) into kinetic energy (KE). Gravitational potential energy is related to the weight (mass times the acceleration of gravity) of the object and the height. Kinetic energy is related to the mass of the object and the speed. Almost all roller coasters start with a lift hill. The lift hill has a motor connected to a chain like a bike chain. This chain pulls the roller coaster car to the top of the hill so it has lots of GPE. The car then rolls freely down the track converting GPE into KE.

Some of the energy is converted into heat through friction. Friction creates heat. Rub your hands together to prove this to yourself. In this roller coaster, you want the maximum amount of friction because you want the lowest kinetic energy as possible at the bottom. Friction depends upon the perpendicular force (normal force) on the rolling object and the two surfaces in contact. The reason the almost horizontal tracks work best for going slow is it gives you the maximum friction. Rough surfaces will also help, so cheap paper towel tubes may actually work best.

Your goal is to go slow, but not stop. This is the opposite of most roller coaster rides at amusement parks. They want speed. That is what makes this such a fun challenge.

Age-Appropriate Engineering

This activity is adjustable for virtually every age. For elementary students, you can use safety scissors; they should cut all the thin cardboard. If you choose to use plastic cups and bottles, start the cuts for the students and let them finish with scissors. Foam cups are a good choice because a hole can easily be made with a pencil.

For middle school students, you can add the math. Gravitational potential energy and kinetic energy formulas are taught at this level. This is also a great age to introduce friction and what affects friction. Friction depends upon the perpendicular force on the rolling object and the two surfaces in contact. As you make the tracks more horizontal, this force goes up, so the amount of friction goes up. And large amounts of friction are the key to winning a slow race.

At the high school level, math is a must. This can even be adapted for the highest levels of physics by discussing the "lost" energy due to friction. The math can be advanced, but they can even calculate the average force of friction for the entire slow run.

Leap of Faith

Create a roller coaster with one or more jumps and a death-defying fall.

Engineering Challenge

For this challenge, select a distance (such as six inches) down the middle of your wall (or foam core) that is not allowed to have any tracks. Use painter's tape to mark the "track free" area. That will force teams to experiment to see where the marble will land after it rolls down one ramp. Experimentation is also needed to create the speed needed to jump the middle gap. At the bottom, you can place a target cup. Hit the target to save the day.

From the Junk Drawer:

- ☐ Painter's tape
- ☐ Foam core, large piece of cardboard, or a wall
- ☐ Paper towel tubes
- ☐ Toilet paper tubes
- ☐ Empty cereal boxes, pasta boxes, etc.
- ☐ Plastic drink bottles, foam cups, etc. (optional)
- ☐ Scissors
- ☐ Plastic cup for target
- ☐ Marble or small rubber ball
- ☐ Paper and pencil for planning

Step 1: Take two long strips of painter's tape and place them down the middle of your board. This is the gap your marble will have to leap over. Use painter's tape to secure the back of the track to the foam core. You can also use a dry erase board, cardboard, or a wall. Painter's tape is easy to reposition and doesn't take paint off the wall.

Step 2: Cut the paper towel tubes and toilet paper tubes lengthwise with scissors. For cereal boxes, cut a strip about 1 inch up from the narrow side of the box. You are going to use the narrow sides as a track to roll the marbles down. With paper and pencil, draw a sketch of your plan. If you are working with a team, brainstorm ideas with your teammates. Brainstorming a good plan is a crucial part of all engineering. Another way is to lay out all of your pieces on a flat tabletop. Move them around to get an awesome looking layout. Some might have to be slightly repositioned to make the roller coaster work, but that is the nature of engineering.

Place your first track on the left side of your board. The angle will have to be a little steep to give the marble enough speed to make the Leap of Faith. The tube should end at the tape line on the left of the board.

Step 3: Test your marble down the first track. Remember, you want it to roll fast enough to jump over whatever gap you are going to have. Use a pencil to mark where it crossed the gap in the other side.

Step 4: Next, create a ramp to catch the marble. Use a marker to draw around the marble at the end of one of your tracks. The line must be larger than the marble.

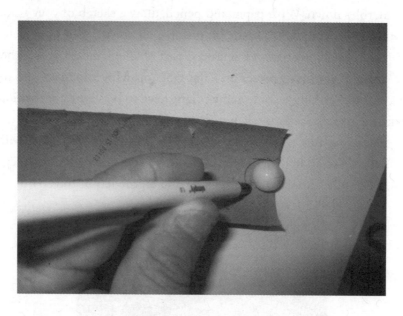

Step 5: Use scissors to cut along this line. This will create a hole for the marble to fall through.

Step 6: Cut a small strip off the end of one of your tubes. Bend this semicircular piece around the end of the ramp where the hole is. You will tape it in a minute, but bend it first to see the shape.

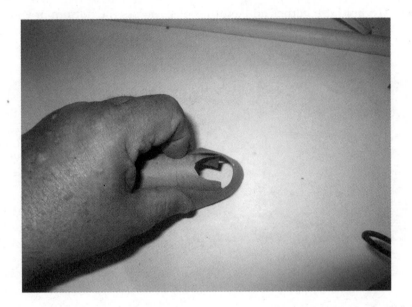

Step 7: Let the curved piece straighten back out and tape one side of it to the outside of your main track.

Step 8: Curve the strip around the end of your main track and secure with tape to the other side.

Step 9: To hold it together, add another piece across the bottom of your main track.

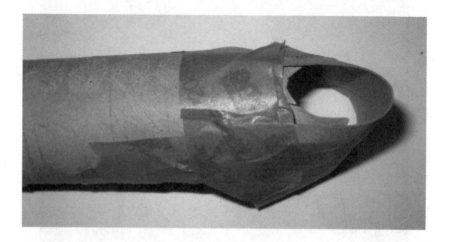

Step 10: Your final piece should look like this. Test that the marble will fall freely through the hole.

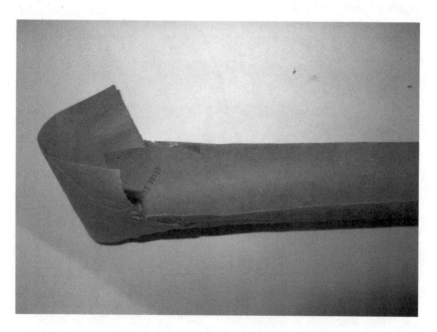

Step 11: Now find the mark where the marble crossed the gap. Place the second track at that mark, going to the right of the tape line.

Step 12: Place a track under the hole in the second track that will direct the marble back toward the gap. Put the marble at the top and test as you go. Make sure you notice where the marble crosses the gap in the middle.

Step 13: Add another track on the other side of the gap that is angled down. If you have enough room, you might add another catch trap like you did earlier, and head back across the gap one more time.

Step 14: Put a cup at the bottom to catch your marble. Let it go from the top and see if you make it! Remember, you can reposition the painter's tape to adjust the ramps if the marble misses anything.

Step 15: If the marble jumps out of the tracks, use your fingers to bend the outside edge of the cardboard toward the mounting surface. This usually needs to be done to make the tracks narrower.

Step 16: Try sending a bunch of marbles down at the same time and enjoy the sights and sounds.

The Science Behind It

In addition to the roller coaster science discussed in Slow Down, the Leap of Faith roller coaster adds projectiles. A projectile is any object that once launched is only under the effects of gravity and air resistance. Baseballs, tennis balls, footballs, and your marble are all projectiles while midair. A rocket, a helicopter, and an airplane are not projectiles since their motors provide an additional force.

All projectiles follow the same curved path called a trajectory. (Air resistance is minor for a marble.) The shape of your trajectory is called a parabola. Hopefully, by observing these parabolas you could adjust your tracks to catch the marble each time. All the while, you are making a leap of faith across the middle of the board.

Age-Appropriate Engineering

For elementary students, you want to use safety scissors. You also want to keep the leap of faith gap small, perhaps only an inch. They can be introduced to projectiles.

For middle schoolers, you want a bigger gap, around four to six inches. Projectiles are easily understood at this age and they should hear the words trajectory, parabola, gravity, and air resistance. A good overall top-to-bottom height at this age is three feet, but that is adjustable depending on the age.

For high school students, projectiles are a commonly taught topic. This engineering activity is fun to do while studying that unit. The vocabulary of projectiles and the math involved is doable for most high schoolers. A great addition at this age is to use a cell phone to videotape the marble as it makes the leap of faith jump. This could even allow them to take measurements and take it to the highest level of physics.

Fridge Run

Use empty plastic bottles and magnets to create the perfect engineering toy for the side of your refrigerator.

Engineering Challenge

Design a Fridge Run using plastic bottles that you can easily reposition over and over. Two groups with the same number of bottles each need to create a successful Fridge Run to win the challenge.

For an advanced challenge, place the starting and ending point at certain fixed locations. After they are placed, they can't move. Now have the young engineers arrange the middle bottles to try to direct the marble from top to bottom. The additional challenge is that you won't give them a marble until they have positioned all of the bottles. Don't let them test it as they go. You could even give them a gold medal if they do it on the first try. If it doesn't work, let them reposition the bottles again (without the marble) and try again. Silver medal this time, if it works. Third try would get a bronze. You could even have fun and make aluminum for fourth place. Add your own medals—just remember that it should be fun to learn.

From the Junk Drawer:

- ☐ 4 to 8 empty plastic bottles that are about the same size (the marble must fit through the mouth of each bottle)
- ☐ Scissors or serrated knife
- ☐ Oven mitt
- ☐ Magnets (strength will determine how many you need)
- ☐ Electrical tape
- ☐ Marble
- ☐ Magnetic attractable surface, like refrigerator door, side, metal filing cabinet side, or most whiteboards

Step 1: If you are using thin water bottles, you can skip to step 4. With adult permission or supervision, use a serrated knife to cut a starting hole near the bottom of an empty plastic bottle. Use an oven mitt to hold the bottle in place and to provide some protection for your hand. For younger children, a parent or adult should make this cut. Most children that can use scissors are OK for the next step.

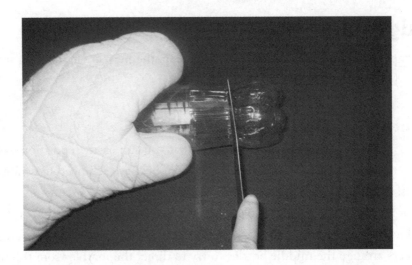

Step 2: Use scissors to finish the cut. Trim the cut part of the bottle so it is as smooth as possible. Remove the labels if they are still on. Don't worry if any residue is left, you can turn that to the back as you add magnets. Set one bottle aside and repeat steps 1 and 2 for remaining bottles.

Step 3: For the bottle you set aside, cut off the top using the method from steps 1 and 2.

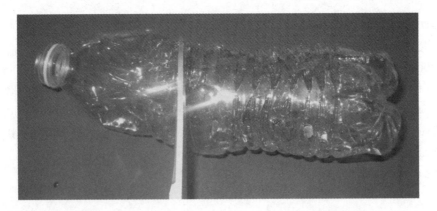

Step 4: If you use the eco-friendly thin plastic bottles, you may not need the serrated knife at all. Just cut across the bottle with a good pair of scissors.

Step 5: If any residue is left from the label, turn this side up. You are going to place at least two magnets (maybe more) on this side. It is important that they are at the same level. Avoid curves in the bottle if possible. Place a magnet on a flat side on top of any residue left.

Step 6: Use a small piece of colored electrical tape to hold the magnet in place. Any tape will work, but the color makes it look better, and this is an engineering project that may be on display in your house or room for a while.

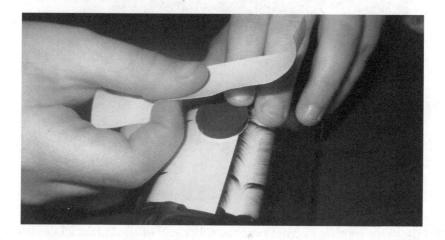

Step 7: Press the tape down, but be careful not to change the shape of the bottle. You want the tape just snug enough to hold the magnet in place.

Step 8: Wrap a longer piece of tape all the way around the bottle. You may be able to combine steps 6, 7, and 8 with one extra-long piece of tape, but two pieces is easier for most people. Also, using scissors with electrical tape is a must, as it doesn't tear very well.

Step 9: Place another magnet near the other end of the bottle. Make sure the magnets are in a straight line, as shown. You want the magnets to be as flat as possible on the surface you are going to race down. Leave room for another magnet between the two in case it is needed. You will test to see if two magnets will work in a few steps.

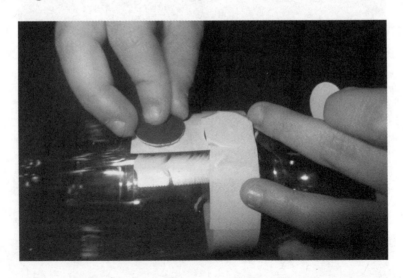

Step 10: Wrap tape around the plastic bottle to hold the second magnet in place. Remember, don't pull the tape so tight you crush the bottle. Also, keep the magnets as flat as possible.

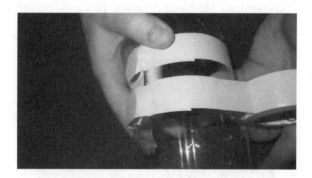

Step 11: Repeat steps 5 through 10 for the other bottles. Leave room for a third magnet (if needed) between the two magnets. You are going to test magnet strength in the next few steps.

Step 12: Place one bottle near the top of your surface. The cut open end needs to be pointing up, and the bottle should be placed at an angle.

Step 13: Add another bottle at an angle under the bottom opening of the first one. Make sure the marble will go in the cut end when dropped. Drop the marble through the top and catch at the opening of the second one. Did the bottles slide down the surface? If they did, you are going to add another magnet in the next two steps. If the bottles stayed in place, you can skip to step 16.

Step 14: If needed, place a third magnet between the first two. Keep all three magnets flat and in a straight line.

Step 15: Wrap tape around the third magnet. You can use the same color or add a different color. It is your Fridge Run, so you get to choose.

Step 16: Add the bottles in any pattern you want. Test it as you add more bottles, unless you are doing the advanced challenges.

Step 17: You can even leave gaps between the bottles and watch the marble jump into each bottle. Regardless of where you make the Fridge Run, putting it on your refrigerator is a great way to let everybody enjoy it. In my high school classroom, there is one that still gets played with on the side of a metal filing cabinet.

Step 18: Move the bottles to new spots and try it again. Enjoy!

The Science Behind It

The Fridge Run is another great way to show energy conversion. At the top, the marble has gravitational potential energy (GPE) because of its mass and height. As the marble falls, the height decreases, so the GPE decreases. But as it falls, the kinetic energy (KE) increases as the speed increases. Eventually almost all of the GPE is converted to KE, so the marble is fastest at the bottom. With the Fridge Run, the speed of the marble is slower than if it had been dropped freely from the same height. The bottles add some friction. Friction steals GPE and turns it into heat. Less GPE is turned into KE, so there is less speed at the bottom. You could drop a second marble from the starting point at the same time as another starts the Fridge Run. The dropped marble is going faster because there is no friction.

Steel is the primary component of refrigerator doors. Steel is a magnetic attractable material. That means magnets will be attracted to it. Most whiteboards also have a metal frame that is made from a magnetic attractable material, so magnets stick to them. Most metals attract magnets, but a few don't. Copper and aluminum are two common metals that don't attract magnets.

You may have to add extra magnets to your bottles because all magnets are not created equal. Most magnets are ceramic magnets, which contain small amounts of magnetic material in a ceramic base. Most of your normal refrigerator magnets use this type. Some magnets are super strong and more expensive. Computer hard drives use this type, usually a neodymium magnet.

Age-Appropriate Engineering

This engineering project is perfect for all ages. For the youngest children, it makes a great toy that you can keep on the side of your refrigerator or a filing cabinet for years.

Upper elementary and middle school students can understand gravitational potential energy being transferred into kinetic energy. Most can also handle the math. This is a good time to explain that some energy is "lost" due to friction. Of course, it has actually been converted into thermal energy.

High school students enjoy this project very much. They finish the construction pretty fast, so they get more time for the math behind the engineering. The Fridge Run can also add in projectiles—try to have the marble jump across big gaps and catch it with the next bottle. High level students can use various tools to measure the exit speed from the last bottle before it is caught. If they know that speed, they can actually figure out exactly how much gravitational potential energy is lost to thermal.

Almost Totally Tubular Roller Coaster

Use pipe wrap to create a homemade roller coaster.

Engineering Challenge

Pipe wrap can be coiled into loops to create even crazier roller coasters tracks. One fun challenge is to create a coaster with at least one loop. Found in home improvement stores, this wrap is designed to insulate water pipes. It is relatively inexpensive. Sold in different sizes, ¾-inch inside diameter usually works well for marbles. All pipe wrap might be slightly different, but you can test and modify your ball choice as part of the engineering activity. Swimming pool noodles will also work, but they are harder to cut since they are thicker. You can keep the pipe wrap for future roller coaster projects once cut.

From the Junk Drawer:

☐ Foam pipe wrap
☐ Marble or small rubber ball
☐ Table and chairs
☐ Painter's tape
☐ Plastic cup for target

Step 1: Pipe wrap already has one long slit, designed to allow the wrap to slide over the pipe. Cut directly across from this slit to create two half-circle tubes. To cut this you will need heavy-duty scissors. Kitchen scissors are a good choice (wash them after cutting the pipe wrap).

Make sure the marble you have chosen will roll easily down the groove in the pipe wrap. If it doesn't, you will have to find a smaller ball.

Step 2: Attach the pipe wrap track to a tabletop. Any tape will work, but painter's tape is the best because it comes off the table and the pipe wrap easily.

Step 3: Attach the pipe wrap track to a chair about a foot away from the edge of the table. The pipe wrap can go all the way to the floor instead if desired. (However, most real roller coasters have flat spots in the middle before falling again.) Wrap a piece of tape over the top and secure to the chair. Test to the see if the marble will roll under the tape. If it hits the tape, go to the next step. If it rolls easily under the tape, you can go to step 5.

Step 4: If the ball hits the tape, loosen one side of the tape. Press the tape down into the open channel of the pipe wrap. Press the outside edges back down to the chair. The marble should then roll freely right over the tape.

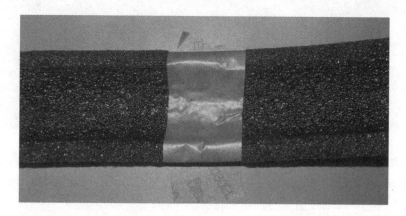

Step 5: To create a loop, coil the other half of pipe wrap into a spiral to see how tight it will wrap. Different pipe wrap will have different densities of foam, so they will coil differently. You need to experiment to decide how tight a loop you can make and what angle the track coming into the loop needs to be. This is best done with two sets of hands. One set of hands should hold the loop and change angles. The other set should let the marble go and grab it at the end. Try different angles and coil sizes until the ball rolls smoothly around the loop.

If you are working alone, you will need to wrap a piece of tape around the loops, as shown. Keep the tape loose enough so that the marble will fit under it. This will allow you to hold the loop with one hand and let the marble go with the other. You may need to make the loop larger if the marble does not roll smoothly. Also, experiment to find the best angle for the loop. Get ready to attach the loop to the first track.

Step 6: Tear off about 6 inches of tape. Press one half of the strip of tape into opposite end of the end of the pipe wrap track that is attached to the table.

Step 7: Butt the end of the loop track to the first track and press the tape down. For a simple two-track section roller coaster, that is probably enough. If you are trying to make a really long one, add more tape to the joint.

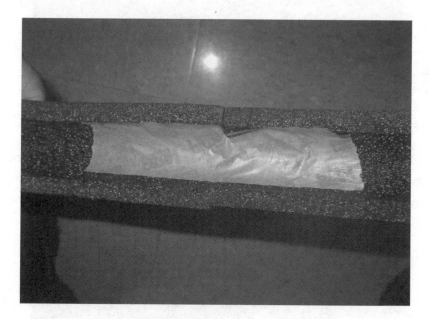

Step 8: You will need to attach the loop to a chair or some type of support to keep it upright.

Step 9: Now you are ready to stand back and admire your Almost Totally Tubular Roller Coaster.

Step 10: Place a cup at the end of your roller coaster to catch the marble.

Step 11: Test the marble and let it go. You can move the supports to modify your design a little. Show your completed roller coaster off to everyone you know. You may also want to change it and try new things. Engineering is about trying new things.

Step 12: Take apart your roller coaster. Painter's tape comes off easily. You can use large rubber bands to keep the pipe wrap together if you want to use it in the future.

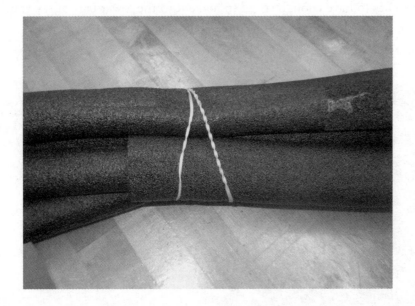

Step 13: If you have a stairwell available, you can build the world's longest Almost Totally Tubular Roller Coaster. Tape all of the available pipe wrap sections together. Then tape the top to the flat floor at the top of the stairs. Run the track down the stairs and curve it at the bottom.

Step 14: Now test it by letting a marble go. You are going to have to tape the track in place at several spots. You may have to move the tape several times to engineer the correct angles to keep the marble in the track. Your marble also has to have enough speed to make it to the lower part of the stairs. If it doesn't, you may need to use a chair at the top of the stairs to create more height.

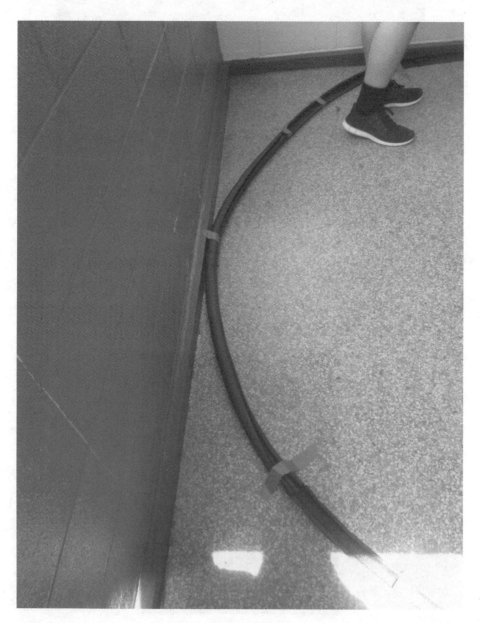

Step 15: Lay the rest of the track down the bottom of the stairs. Tape it in place. Test it out. Move the tape if needed. Once it works, show it off to everybody. You could keep going if you have a multiple story stairwell and enough pipe wrap. Have fun!

The Science Behind It

Roller coasters are, at their heart, a conversion from gravitational potential energy to kinetic energy. Almost all roller coasters keep going downhill, but occasionally they go uphill. The first, tallest hill is called the drop hill. After that the track will rise up to another shorter hill. As the coaster car climbs it loses speed but it gains gravitational potential energy. The car then drops and repeats the cycle with each hill getting progressively shorter as the car loses energy to friction.

With pipe wrap, you can simulate this up-and-down motion. As long as the hills get smaller, you can just keep going. All roller coasters worked the same way until the introduction of steel roller coasters. Steel roller coasters could bend, twist, and even roll because the cars were held onto the track by wheels on the underside of the track. Steel roller coaster cars can't fall off.

With pipe wrap, you can also create loops. But since your marble is not hooked to the track, you need to experiment to find the right angle to create enough speed to get around the loop. Objects move in a circle because of centripetal force. Centripetal force is present anytime an object turns. This force depends upon speed, mass, and **radius** of the turn. The correct angle is needed to get the speed. The mass is your marble. You can coil the pipe wrap until you find a radius that works. It takes a lot of practice, but that is what engineers do. They try something until they get it right. Real-world steel roller coasters have an advantage because of the underside wheels, so what you are doing to create a loop is harder.

Age-Appropriate Engineering

For elementary age students, an adult will have to cut the pipe wrap. Loops may not be appropriate except for upper elementary grades. A discussion of potential and kinetic energy is also age-appropriate for upper elementary students.

For middle school and high school students, there is almost no limit to this except for the number of pieces of pipe wrap they get. You can also add math and have them calculate the initial gravitational potential energy. With the use of a cell phone video recorder, you can even record the speed at the bottom. This speed would allow you to calculate the kinetic energy at the bottom. The difference between these numbers would be the "lost" energy due to friction.

Mint Can Challenge

Investigate how distributing weights in a can will change how an object rolls.

Engineering Challenge

Place weights inside a mint can so it rolls the fastest down a ramp. The challenge can also be to roll the mint cans the slowest down a ramp.

As with almost all the engineering projects in this book, the pictures and instructions will show you how to do it one way. For a true inquiry-based experiment, hand the materials out and let the future engineers experiment.

From the Junk Drawer:

- ☐ 2 identical round mint cans
  (Ice Breakers mint containers work
  well)
- ☐ Tape
- ☐ 8 to 12 equal weights
- ☐ Ramp
- ☐ Ruler
- ☐ 2 identical soup cans, one cream-
  based and one broth-based
  (optional)

Step 1: Remove the top of the mint can. Any shallow, round can will do as
long as the sides are smooth. (Note: This can be done with tuna fish or pet
food cans, but only if you use a safety can opener. Safety can openers cut
around the edge of the can lid so that there are no leftover sharp edges to
cut fingers. Plastic round jar lids without a lip also work, but you can't hide
the weights. It is important that the sides be smooth so the cans will roll in
a straight line.)

Step 2: Roll a small piece of tape so the sticky side faces out and use it to secure one weight to the inside surface of the outside rim of a mint can, as shown.

Step 3: Repeat for a total of either four or six weights. Space the weights evenly around the inside edge. If you are using a mint can, put the top back on.

Step 4: Roll a slightly larger piece of tape and secure it to the middle of the lid of the other can. Place the same number of weights as in the previous can. This time you want to put all the weights on the tape in the center. Place the weights in a tight, symmetrical pattern, as shown below.

Step 5: Incline the ramp using books or other available stackable objects. Any angle will work, but you probably don't want to start super steep.

Step 6: Stand the cans up on edge and hold them in place with a ruler.

Step 7: Quickly pull the ruler out and observe which can rolls faster. Experiment with placing the weights in different locations inside the can.

Step 8: Another way to see the same concept is to use two soup cans. Use a broth-based soup like chicken noodle and a cream-based soup like cream of mushroom. Try to use the same brand so that you know the cans are the same size diameter. Put both at the top of the ramp and hold them in place with a ruler.

Step 9: Let the ruler go and watch what happens. You can try again if you want. You could even experiment with different cans of vegetables to see that not all things roll equally.

The Science Behind It

You are probably familiar with a science topic called inertia. Inertia is the tendency of an object to maintain the same state of motion. Inertia is directly related to the mass of an object. A big truck is harder to start moving than a small car. And a big truck is also harder to stop moving because of the large mass of the truck.

How an object spins is related to a quantity engineers call moment of inertia. Moment of inertia tells how easily an object rotates. It is very similar to regular inertia but moment of inertia only deals with spinning objects. Moment of inertia depends upon the mass and how the mass is distributed for the spinning object.

A way that you can see this in practice is by watching figure skating. At some point in every routine, figure skaters will start spinning. They will spin at a certain speed. They pull their arms in across their chests and will spin crazy fast. Their mass doesn't change, but as they pull their arms in they can spin easier. Easier spinning means faster spinning. You also see it in diving and gymnastics. As gymnasts and divers curl into balls, they rotate faster. As they straighten their bodies, it slows their rotation and allows them to make a perfect landing.

Another way to see moment of inertia is by looking at car tires. When your parents buy tires, the tires are balanced. Tires are balanced by adding masses at certain locations on the outside edge of the metal part of the rim. On many vehicles you can see these, but sometimes they are under a hubcap. Go look at your car tires and see if you can find them.

Moment of inertia is a fun engineering topic and is crucial for all spinning objects. Learning about moment of inertia can possibly lead to a career in race car design, gymnastics, or just about anything that spins.

Age-Appropriate Engineering

This engineering activity is useful for just about any age, but is not usually taught even in high school. However, all ages can understand the concept. You could use it as a great hook to get athletic students motivated at almost every level. Since everything you are dealing with is safe, this activity is fun for all.

One extension you can add uses a spinning office chair. Have a student sit in the office chair with two weights in his hands (like soup cans or small dumbbells). Spin the student. As he extends his arms, he will slow down. As he pulls his arms in across his chest, he will spin faster. Extended arms raises the moment of inertia so he spins slower. Pulling his arms in lowers his moment of inertia so he spins faster. Just be careful how fast the student spins so he stays safely on the chair.

Windmill Challenge

Harness the power of the wind as you create homemade windmills. Lift weights to determine who is the Champion of the Windmills.

Engineering Challenge

Create a windmill to lift a weight. Windmill power is one of the keys to meet our future energy needs. Build a simple windmill and use it to lift weights. There are many ways to make this work. What follows is one example, as well as a few pictures of other styles.

From the Junk Drawer:

☐ Foam cups
☐ Tape
☐ Wooden skewers
☐ Plastic drink bottles with plastic caps
☐ Scissors and a serrated knife
☐ Marker
☐ Hammer and small nail
☐ Fan

☐ Plastic cups
☐ Thin string or thread
☐ Stopwatch or cell phone
☐ Small washers or any lightweight object to lift
☐ Small plastic condiment cups (optional)
☐ Small metal peanut can (optional)
☐ Heavy paper (optional)

Step 1: Put a weight inside a foam cup. This is just to give the base stability. Place another cup on top of the foam cup and tape the two together. This will form the base of the windmill.

Step 2: Stick a wooden skewer through the side of the top cup. This will be the rotating shaft of the windmill.

Step 3: Cut the bottom off a rinsed-out plastic drink bottle. Thin plastic water bottles work well and usually can be cut with scissors. Thicker bottles will need an adult to start the cut with a serrated knife and then it can be finished with scissors.

Step 4: With a marker, draw a line straight up the bottle. Repeat for the opposite side of the bottle. Turn the bottle a quarter turn and repeat. Your finished bottle should have four equal parts with lines separating the parts. Cut along those lines up to the neck of the bottle. The lines helps make sure the blades are close in size.

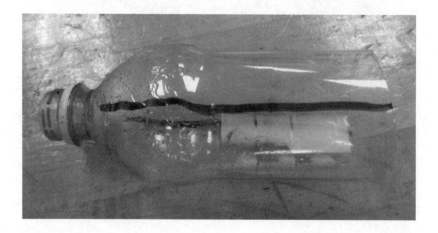

Step 5: Bend all four blades back so it looks like a fan, as shown.

Step 6: Use your fingers to curve the blades. All blades need to be curved the same direction. You can curve them more later, if desired.

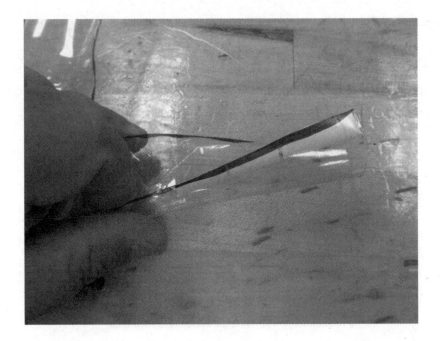

Step 7: Hold up the fan and make sure the blades are bent about an equal
distance.

Step 8: Locate the center of the top part of the plastic cap with a nail.

Step 9: If you haven't already, take the cap off the bottle. Use a hammer to
lightly tap the nail through the cap. Make sure the surface under the cap is
safe to be hit by a nail. Use a stack of old magazines if you are unsure.

Step 10: Wiggle the nail around to make the hole a little bigger.

Step 11: Slide the pointed end of the wooden skewer through the top of the cap. You want it to be very tight. Wiggle the nail around to make the hole larger if necessary.

Step 12: Screw the cap of the bottle back onto the cut bottle.

Step 13: Replace the wooden skewer in the base of the windmill with the wooden skewer still attached to your bottle cap. Now you have a working windmill! It's time to test it. Place a fan in front of your windmill and turn the fan on. You might want to start on low and increase the speed later. You can use a blow dryer with the heat turned off if you don't have a fan.

Step 14: Now create an object to lift. A small plastic cup with a string taped across the top is perfect way to hold the objects because it will allow you to easily change the weight to be lifted. Tie a long piece of string to the string across the top.

Step 15: Use a small piece of tape to attach the other end of the string to the back of the skewer.

Step 16: Twist the skewer until the string is tight while the cup is still resting on the surface.

Step 17: Turn on the fan and watch the cup rise as the skewer rotates. You might want to try different fan speeds. If you are having a contest, time the rise of the cup using a cell phone. Try bending the blades more or less to see if you can make it climb faster. Next, try different small objects as weights in the cup.

A Few Other Methods

Here are a few other windmill blade styles that all use the same basic windmill base and skewer.

Step 18: A waterwheel-style windmill made using small cups is another easy and fun way to lift the weight.

Step 19: The style shown below uses the bottom of a peanut can for the blades. The metal is thin enough to be cut with scissors. The edges will be sharp, so be careful as you bend the blades.

Step 20: If you can fold a ninja star out of paper, it makes a great windmill. Bend each wing of the star slightly to help it spin.

Step 21: Cutting a plastic cup with three spiral slices is a wonderful propeller. Fold the three pieces out and the natural curve of the cup will spin like crazy.

The Science Behind It

Windmills are one of the oldest engineering devices known to man. They have been pumping water for years. In the last few years, they have started becoming a great, clean way to generate electricity. Wind has energy. Turning that energy into electricity or lifting weights is a perfect way to get cheap energy. Of course, we used a fan to create the wind. But if you take your windmill outside, you get free energy into your windmill by using wind.

Age-Appropriate Engineering

For younger children, creating the windmill and getting it to spin should be enough. The windmill allows you to discuss energy and where we get it from.

For middle school students, this is a great challenge and a great way to talk about converting energy. Energy converters like this are objects we use all the time. Radios turn electricity into sound. Lights turn electricity into light. Windmills are just another example of this. Students of this age can calculate the potential energy gained by lifting the weight.

For high schoolers, math can be extended. With the right equipment, you can measure the electrical energy into the fan. If you calculate the output potential energy, you can then calculate efficiency.

This is a fun activity for all ages, and students will get really creative. Encourage that and enjoy the Windmill Challenge.

$g = 10 \, m/sec^2$

$E = \frac{1}{2} mv^2$

potential
energy

$S = \frac{d}{t}$

$W = mg$

torque

force
area

$F = ma$

pressure $= \frac{force}{area}$

$f = \frac{1}{T}$

2

Structures

People have been building structures since humans first left caves. They have built structures to live in, to hold things, and to do things. Engineers are the designers for the structures we use today. They build them and test them to keep everybody safe.

Now it's time for you to build structures to learn about science and engineering.

Index Card Textbook Challenge

How many books can you stack on a single index card?

Engineering Challenge

Using only scissors and a single index card, elevate as many textbooks as possible off a tabletop. Tape can be used if desired, but this challenge works just as well without it. The rules can be modified to include a minimum height above the table. Half an inch is a good height. If you fail to include a height at least one enterprising student will just lay the card on the table and start stacking textbooks. When that happened in my classroom I had to declare that group the winner. Contest rules are meant to be stretched, but you want to reward creativity.

From the Junk Drawer:

☐ Ruler

☐ Index cards (any size is acceptable)

☐ Pencil

☐ Scissors

☐ Tape (optional)

☐ Textbooks (any books will work)

Step 1: Use a ruler to measure 1-inch intervals along the long side of an index card.

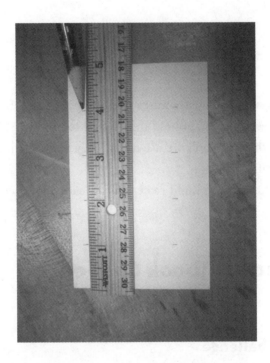

Step 2: Use a pencil to draw lines across the card at each 1-inch mark.

Step 3: Use scissors to cut along the lines. This will create equal 1-inch strips. The number of strips will depend upon the size of the index card.

Step 4: Fold each of the pieces in half lengthwise to create a piece of "angle iron."

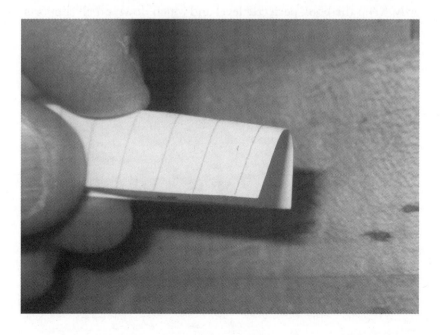

Step 5: Use your fingernail to crease the edges of your angle irons.

Step 6: Carefully stand up your supports in a rectangle slightly smaller than the book you are going to use. Add the remaining strips in the middle for added support.

Step 7: Carefully lower the first book onto the columns. You want to do this slowly. Keep the book perfectly level and touch down on all supports at the same time.

Step 8: Slowly lower another book on top of the previous book. Keep adding books one at a time until you have a gigantic collapse. Of course, you are only using an index card, so eventually your design will fail. But watching it collapse is fun.

Challenge Option Two

Step 9: Fold an index card in half, hamburger style.

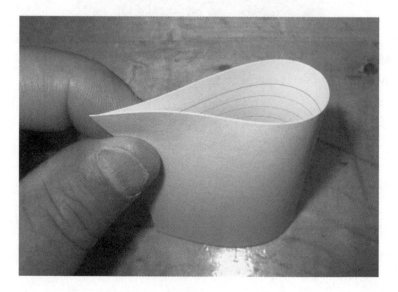

Step 10: Use a thumbnail to crease along the fold.

Step 11: Use scissors to cut the card in half.

Step 12: Fold one of the pieces in half and crease the fold.

Step 13: Fold one of the sides back, as shown. Crease the fold with a thumbnail to make it sharp.

Step 14: Turn it over and repeat for the other side. You should end up with an accordion fold, as shown.

Step 15: Repeat steps 12 to 14 with the other half of the index card. Stand the two pieces up. The distance apart should be smaller than the book you are trying to support.

Step 16: Gently lower the book onto the index card. It is important that the book comes straight down and hits both supports at the same time. Add more books until it all comes crashing down, or leave it standing and show it off.

The Science Behind It

The strength of the index card supports in this project comes from their shape. Construction engineers use I-beams all the time. The angled beams provide excellent strength. Since they are thin but bent, they use less material. Box beams and angle iron are other shapes that give good strength and save material. And saving materials allow engineers to save money. Saving raw materials is also good for the environment.

Paper has a surprising amount of strength when pulled or pushed along the longest direction. Lying flat, almost anything would bend it. But roll it up and it is incredibly strong in the long direction. You can also gain massive amounts of strength by folding it with an accordion fold. This same fold is what you see at the center of corrugated cardboard that makes it strong.

Stability is also an issue when building any structure. The supports need to be placed toward the edge and spread out. This gives your structure a wider base and makes it more stable. Construction and civil engineers design buildings all the time using the same principles you just used.

Age-Appropriate Engineering

For the very young, simply getting your Index Card Challenge to support one or two thin books is cause to celebrate. At that age, they need to succeed and have fun. Competitions can be left to older students.

For upper elementary and middle school students, the designs should get better and stronger. You can even introduce the concept of strength-to-weight ratio of the legs. Since the total force down is supported by the legs, the little engineers can calculate the force on each leg.

For high school students, they can calculate force on each leg and also be taught about conditions for static equilibrium. Designing like this is at the heart of structural and civil engineering. But most of all, watching this age student laugh when their Index Card Challenge collapses is a joy to behold. The joy of watching destruction never gets old. It is always amazing to watch 17-year-olds giggling like toddlers.

Newspaper Table

Build a table from a daily newspaper.

Engineering Challenge

Build a table out of newspaper that will hold up a book. The rule my class uses for height is that my hand has to slide underneath it. Another good rule is that the table must be freestanding (it cannot be secured to a wall or the like). Prior to building your Newspaper Table, it is a good idea to brainstorm and draw a plan. But you can experiment as you go if you choose. Your choice may depend on how much newspaper you have. In my class, the students are required to create a plan first. This is an attempt to minimize one student dominating the group. For a classroom contest, you also want each group to have the same amount of newspaper and masking tape.

Any newspaper size will work, as shown. The first table is created using a traditional newspaper size. The second table is made using smaller newspaper like the free weeklies that many areas have. For a larger group, you can ask your local newspaper for copies of the old newspapers that didn't sell. You can also have students bring in old newspapers and get them involved. Students love to help. The best part is that all of the leftovers can be recycled after you remove the tape.

From the Junk Drawer:

☐ Newspaper
☐ Scissors
☐ Masking tape (or clear tape)
☐ Flat piece of cardboard (optional)
☐ Books or magazines to test your table

Option A: Basic Table Design

Step 1: Fold a traditional size newspaper in half, hot dog style. Make sure the corners are even and then use your thumbnail to create a crease.

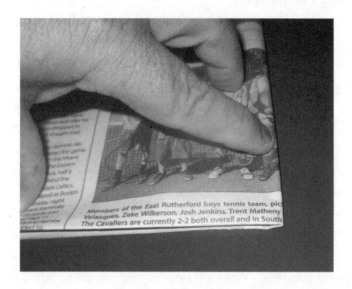

Step 2: Use scissors to cut along the crease. You can trim the edges after you are done if needed. The cut has to be fairly straight, but a little off is OK.

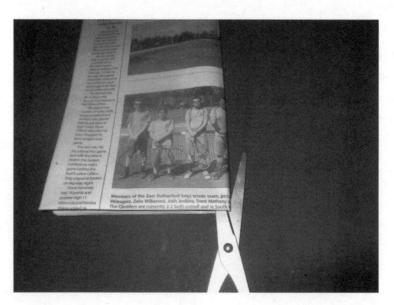

Step 3: Starting at the fold of the paper, roll it up. The roll doesn't have to be super tight. It actually stands easier if it is not too tight. These rolls are going to be the legs of your table.

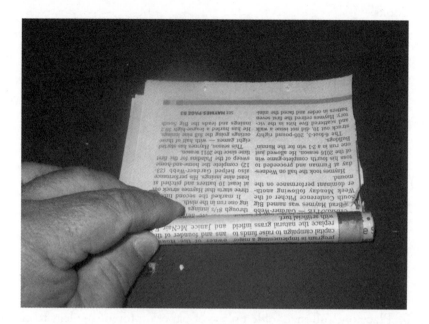

Step 4: Use a 1-inch piece of tape to hold the roll together.

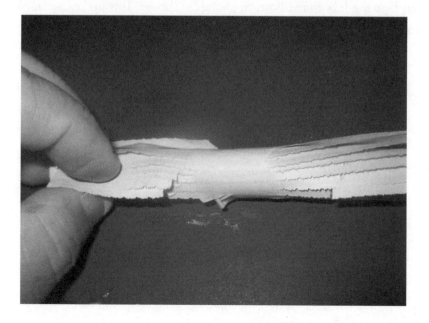

Step 5: Stand the rolls up to form the four corner legs of your table. You can add a fifth leg directly in the middle if you want additional strength. Five legs is the way to go if you are going to try to hold up the greatest number of books.

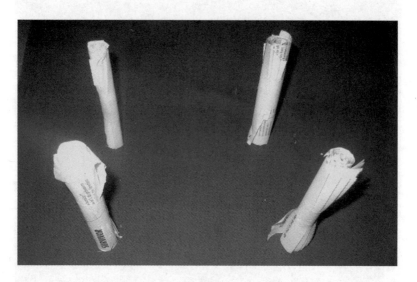

Step 6: Place one full-size folded piece of paper on top of the legs to create a tabletop. You can also use a piece of cardboard. If you use cardboard, you can tape the legs to the bottom of the cardboard. This makes a completely portable table that the students could take home and actually use.

Step 7: Gently place a book on top of the table. Try stacking more if you want, or try to make a stack tall enough to reach the ceiling. Just place each book gently as you add it.

Option B: One of the Strongest Newspaper Tables Ever

Step 8: This was done with one of the smaller, weekly-sized newspapers, but it could be done with any size. Pull off one single page. Fold the single page in half. Starting at one end, roll it up into a tight tube. For this style, a tighter leg will probably help. Use a very small piece of tape to hold it together.

Step 9: Pull out six pieces and put them aside. One is for the tabletop, unless you are using cardboard. The other five will be used in the next step. Roll all of the remaining single remaining sheets in your newspaper into tubes.

Step 10: Fold one of the pieces you pulled out earlier in half so it is the same height as the tubes. Wrap this piece around five or six tubes and secure with a small piece of tape. The number inside each leg can vary depending on how many tubes you have. You want all five legs about equal in diameter. It is OK if a few of the legs have more tubes inside.

Step 11: Stand up four legs slightly smaller than the dimension of the books you are going to use. You can use your eyeball as long as you are close.

Step 12: Stand a fifth leg up in the middle for additional support.

Step 13: Place your last folded piece of newspaper on top for the tabletop. Like before, you can use cardboard and tape the legs to the underside of the cardboard tabletop. You just can't tape the legs to the worktable.

Step 14: Gently place one book on top of your Newspaper Table.

Step 15: Place a few more, but be gentle as you set them down. Sideways
   motion is not wanted, so bring the books straight down, touching all parts
   of the book at the same time.

Step 16: Now is a good time to test the correct height with the agreed upon measuring device. This can be 4 inches (or a similar measurement), but I just use my hand standing up.

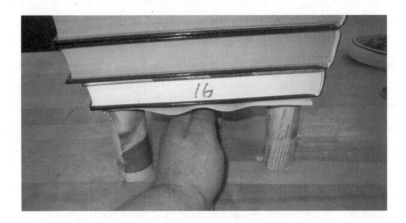

Step 17: Keep stacking. Be careful to keep students away as it gets very tall. One time, we stacked every textbook in my classroom on it—over 40. We left it overnight, but the next day textbooks littered my floor. The cause of the collapse was probably humidity. Don't leave a really big stack overnight!

The Science Behind It

These paper tables work because the weight is spread equally among the four (or sometimes five) legs. The cardboard tabletop is stronger, and if you are building one for your house, that is the way to go. You could actually use a piece of wood for the top and add more tape to the legs and create a table you could use for years to come.

Rolling the paper up into legs shows you the power of a tube. Tubes are incredibly strong when the force is applied to the skinny end. Many tubes are weak, though, if you push on them from the side. Try it with an empty toilet paper tube. Press with both hands on the opposite ends and it's pretty strong. This is called compression strength since you are trying to compress the tube. It's amazingly strong. But if you push in the middle, the tube buckles. This is called a shear force, and tubes do not handle that very well.

Putting several smaller tubes together is a way to make your table drastically stronger. The cable that holds up the Golden Gate Bridge is created that way for the same reason. It uses a bunch of individual cables that are braided together. You can't braid your paper tubes, but binding them together makes the table stronger. It is also much easier to roll the individual small tubes than it would be to roll a fat tube.

On each table leg, you also have to worry about the pressure. Pressure is force divided by area. The total force is the sum of all the books and tabletop. The force is split between all of the legs. A bigger area has less pressure. The larger tube legs have more area, so they can handle larger forces. A steak knife cutting into the skin of a potato can create more pressure than an elephant's foot. The knife has a smaller force, but the knife blade has an incredibly tiny area. The elephant has a much larger force, but it is spread out over a gigantic foot. An elephant in high heels would stab the heels into the dirt and wouldn't be able to walk. Have you ever seen an elephant in high-heeled shoes?

Age-Appropriate Engineering

Since you are only using scissors, this is safe for all ages. Be careful if the book stacks get too tall. For young elementary age students, use smaller books. If the table just supports one book, that's fine. You may want to introduce pressure if they are advanced.

For upper elementary and middle school students, you can introduce pressure and the importance of the tube. You can also do the toilet paper tube trick to teach them about compression forces and shear forces. You can even have them calculate the pressure on each leg. Just assume all legs have equal force pushing down.

For high school students, you probably want to add the pressure math part. You may even encourage them to research ways to make the table even stronger. This can be done by adding cross braces and new materials.

Paper Tower

Using a single sheet of copy paper and 25 centimeters of tape, create the tallest freestanding tower possible.

Engineering Challenge

All groups must create a freestanding Paper Tower that is taller than a single sheet of paper. The contest leader must give some contest rules, and these can be flexible. The biggest thing to stress is that the tower has to stand for a certain amount of time. A good contest rule for standing time is 10 seconds. That allows the tower to be built lying down, and adds a little drama and fun as the teams stand it up. For a graded assignment, a teacher can give each team a grade for reaching a certain height and reward extra credit to the tallest tower. A teacher could even give creativity or style points for different designs. Here are two designs: one that will guarantee success for younger children, and one that reaches for the sky but takes more dexterity.

From the Junk Drawer:

☐ Single sheet of copy paper
☐ Scissors
☐ Transparent tape (for a contest, all teams should get the same amount)
☐ Pencil
☐ Wooden dowel and skewer (for second option)
☐ Ruler
☐ Paper cutter (optional)

Option 1: For Smaller Hands

Step 1: Fold a piece of paper in half. Make sure you match the corners up perfectly. This can be done either hot dog style or hamburger style. For the younger kids, hamburger style is easier to roll into a tube later. Repeat the fold again to create a folded piece of paper with four equal-size folds.

Step 2: Use scissors to cut along the folds.

Step 3: You are going to create a large paper tube. Roll one strip of paper into a long roll. The roll does not have to be super small as long as it forms a tube. Use a very small piece of tape to secure the middle and both ends.

Step 4: Stack three of the tubes up in a triangle. Use a long piece of tape to wrap around one end. Do not crush any of the tubes as you wrap the tape around the end.

Step 5: Stand the three taped tubes up, as shown. Depending on the size of the tubes, this may take patience, but you can do it.

Step 6: Balance the fourth tube on top of the triangle. You have just created a tower taller than a single sheet of paper. You can use small pieces of tape to help secure it, if the top tube falls off.

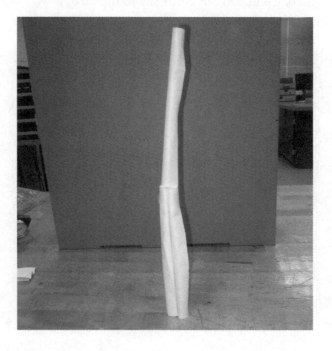

Option 2: For Older Students

Step 7: To create a taller tower, you will need to create smaller tubes of paper. Use a ruler to mark every 1 inch along both short sides of a piece of copy paper.

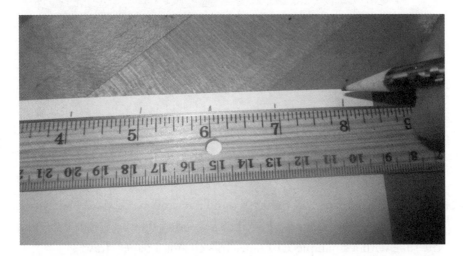

Step 8: Use a pencil and the ruler to connect the lines across the sheet of paper.

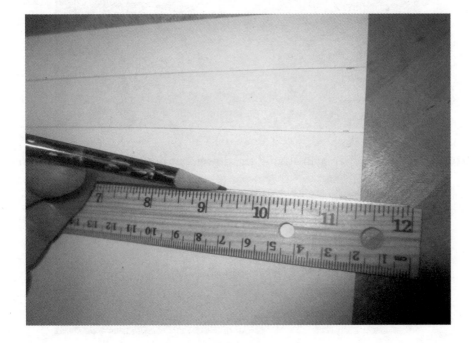

Step 9: Using scissors, cut along the lines. This will create eight 1-inch strips from a standard sheet of copy paper and you will have a narrow strip leftover.

Step 10: Roll a 1-inch strip tightly around a narrow wood dowel lengthwise. You can also roll it around a pencil or a wooden skewer. Secure each end of the tube with a small piece of tape. This creates a paper straw.

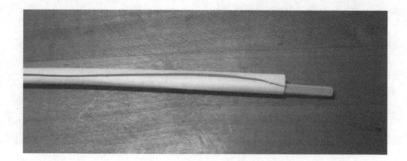

Step 11: Roll another strip around the dowel, but don't tape the roll this time.

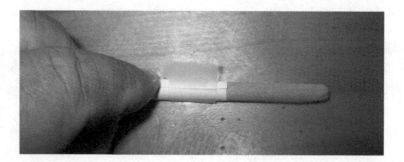

Step 12: Slide the taped paper straw about 1 inch inside the untaped paper straw. Use a small piece of tape to join the two straws. This creates a long straw almost 20 inches long. Repeat steps 10 through 12 to create three long straws. These will form a tripod for the base of your tower.

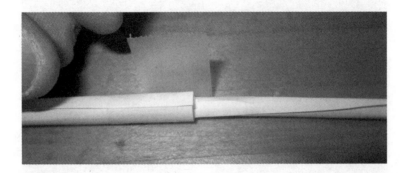

Step 13: Using a small piece of tape, tape the ends of all three tubes together. The three ends should form a small triangle.

Step 14: The next steps are not required but will make your tripod sturdier. Use the narrow strip of paper left over from earlier. Wrap it tightly around the dowel.

Step 15: Continue wrapping until you have a small, fat straw.

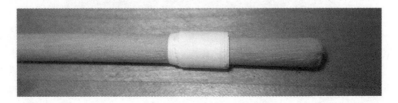

Step 16: Stand your tripod up. Move the legs out until the tripod is very stable. Slide the fat straw in the bottom middle of the tripod. This will help keep the three legs spread out in a tripod shape.

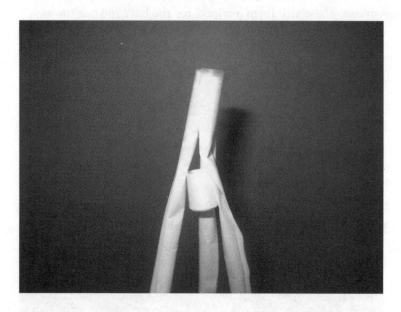

Step 17: Stand the tripod up and adjust the short fat straw so it stays upright.

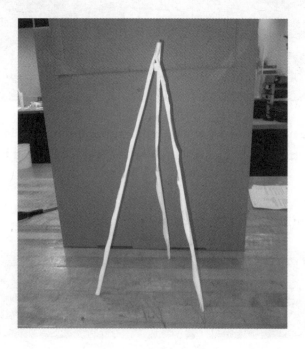

Step 18: From the tripod base, you will create a single long pole for the top. This pole is best created on a flat surface. Then stand it up after you complete it. For a very stable tower, you can continue making straws, as shown earlier. The straws should be rolled as tightly as possible to save paper. If the rules state that the tower must stand for minimum amount of time, wait until the judge comes to stand the tower up when you're finished. Finally, stand it up and enjoy the sense of accomplishment.

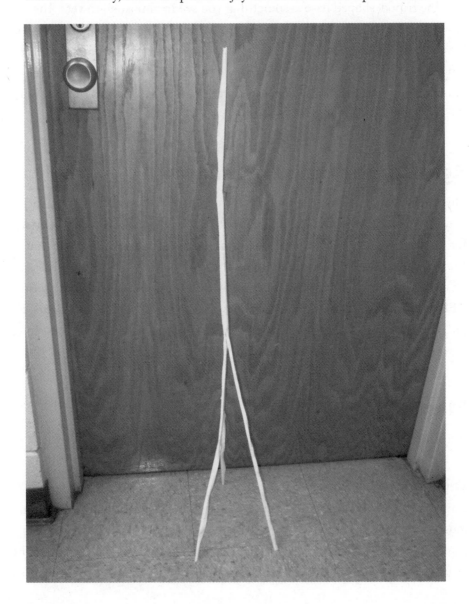

The Science Behind It

Building taller structures has been an engineering goal since all engineers wore fur. The keys to a tall structure are a good base and thoughtful use of materials. You can look at cell phone and radio antennas to see what is possible if you keep building paper towers. Of course, eventually you might switch to steel or other materials, but the engineering is the same.

The tripod-shaped base is something you see in almost all towers. The Eiffel Tower has a four-legged base, but it is similar in design to what you may have just built. Adding a fourth leg is important to make it stronger and last longer. Your tower only has to stand for a few minutes to be measured. Cell phone towers and the Eiffel Tower are stronger to stand the test of time, but the engineering concepts are the same.

Age-Appropriate Engineering

This engineering challenge is remarkably similar for all ages. Older students may get more creative and build taller towers. Creating a solid tripod is vital for the younger set. They may only get a tripod and one member above that. But they are still getting the hang of it.

For older kids, a time limit is a great way to promote teamwork. This is a Phun Physics Phriday challenge that I still do with high school students. I give the students 10 minutes to design and 10 minutes to build. The best tower always comes from the team that works the best together.

Marshmallow Tower

Build a freestanding tower using toothpicks and marshmallows.

Engineering Challenge

Build a support structure using only marshmallows and toothpicks. The dome must be able to support a tennis ball or some other agreed upon weight. You could also make a challenge to see which group's tower holds the most weight, or let everyone win if it holds a certain amount of weight. It is probably a good idea to limit the number of toothpicks and marshmallows for each group. A good starting point is 15 toothpicks and 15 marshmallows per group.

Another engineering option is to make stability a factor by creating a tower that will withstand the high winds from a multispeed fan—the tower must stand upright while the wind is blowing.

From the Junk Drawer:

☐ Pencil and paper

☐ Toothpicks

☐ Marshmallows (large marshmallows are the easiest to use)

☐ Tennis ball or other small weights

☐ Multispeed fan (optional)

Step 1: Brainstorm ideas before starting to build. Draw a sketch of the design on paper. If working with a group, get input from all team members. Almost all engineering projects start with a brainstorming and design process. A sketch is crucial before attempting to build projects. You can always modify your design later if needed. As with any engineering design, there are many ways to build this project. The pictures show one way. Be creative!

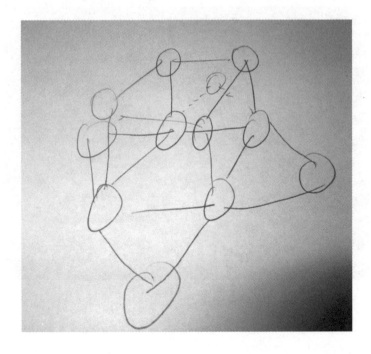

Step 2: Build the base by creating a square of marshmallows. First push one end of the toothpick into a marshmallow.

Step 3: Push the other end into another marshmallow.

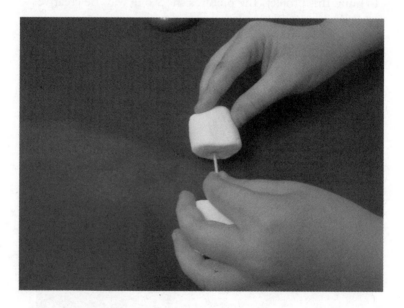

Step 4: Push a toothpick into one marshmallow at a right angle to the original toothpick, and put another marshmallow on the other end. Repeat that step to make a square of marshmallows.

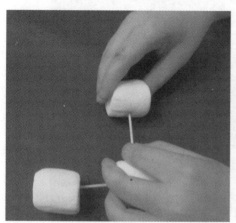
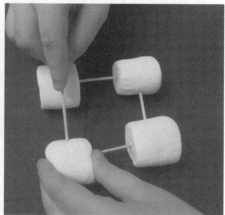

Step 5: Complete another square using marshmallows and toothpicks.

Step 6: Push a toothpick into one corner of one square perpendicular to the other toothpicks.

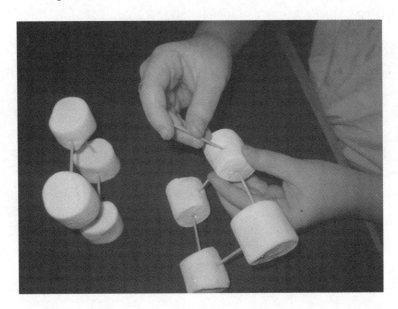

Step 7: Place the other square standing up and push the other end of the toothpick into the second square, as shown. The squares should stand freely after that.

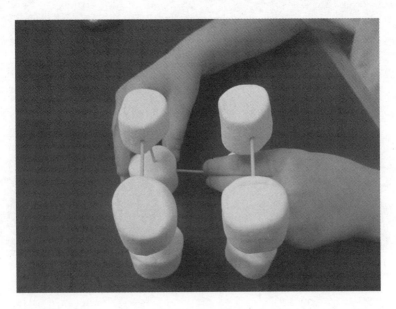

Step 8: Repeat for the other side of the base. You can slightly pull the marshmallows apart on one side to push the toothpicks into both marshmallows on the other side.

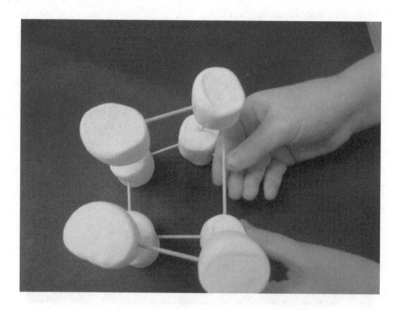

Step 9: Repeat for the top of the two squares. You should end up with a cube with marshmallows at each corner.

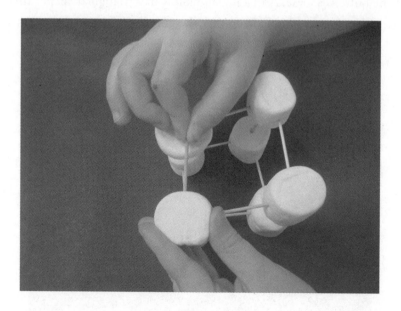

Step 10: Now it is time to test the strength of your Marshmallow Tower. Gently place a tennis ball on top. Another option is to place an index card on the top of the tower and use a small weight in the center of the index card (like a keychain or washer).

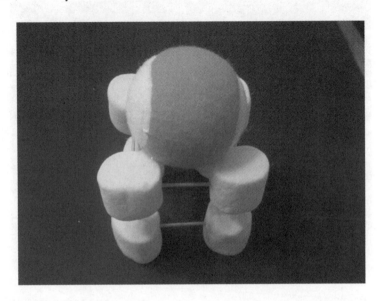

Step 11: To make the tower more stable, push two toothpicks into one side of the bottom square. Add a marshmallow in a triangular shape. This triangular shape will help keep the Marshmallow Tower strong and steady.

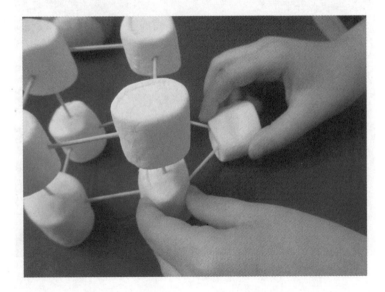

Step 12: Repeat step 11 for all four sides. This will make the base stronger and more stable.

Step 13: Test the tower again by placing the tennis ball on top.

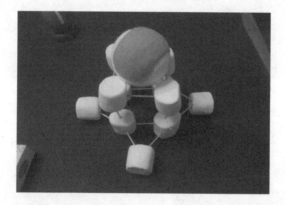

Step 14: Build another square by repeating steps 2 through 4.

Step 15: Place a toothpick standing up in each corner of the top square of
your existing tower. Push the toothpick almost all the way through the
marshmallow for maximum strength.

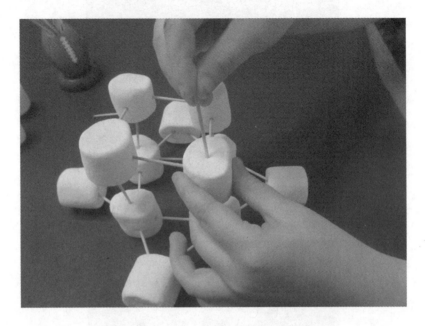

Step 16: Push the new square onto the top of the toothpicks you just inserted
to create a third level.

Step 17: Test it by placing the tennis ball on top. Look at your design and see what you could do to improve it. You could take it apart and build another to try and make it stronger.

Step 18: If you want to go higher and have limited numbers of marshmallows, you can build a triangular tower. Build a triangle for the base similar to the way you made the square earlier.

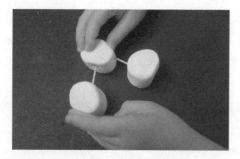

Step 19: Push a toothpick into each corner of the bottom triangle standing straight up.

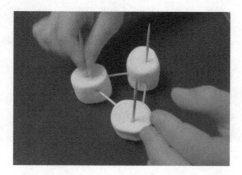

Step 20: Push a marshmallow down onto each standing toothpick you just put in.

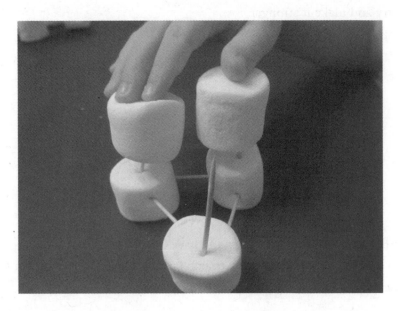

Step 21: Put a toothpick between each marshmallow in the top triangle. Remember that you can slightly pull the marshmallows apart to put the toothpick in and then push them back to the correct position.

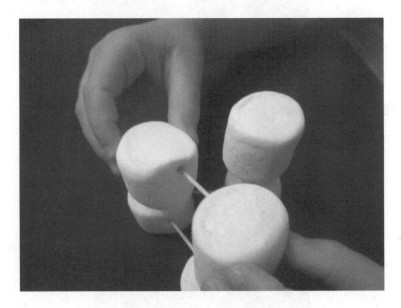

Step 22: Place the tennis ball on top to test your tower.

Step 23: Add extra support to your base by adding a toothpick and marshmallow coming out from each corner. This is especially important if you are going to wind test it with a fan.

Step 24: It is time to test it again. Gently place the tennis ball on top. After that, you can add another level or two if the highest tower is your goal.

Step 25: Purely for fun, try to recreate the Leaning Tower of Pisa with marshmallows and toothpicks. Try to get it to stand for 10 seconds. Good luck. The real Leaning Tower of Pisa is attached to the ground so it has stood for many years. The ground started sinking under one side almost as soon as work was started. Engineers stabilized the ground under the real tower a few years ago. They probably could straighten it out if desired, but the citizens of Pisa love their leaning tower too much.

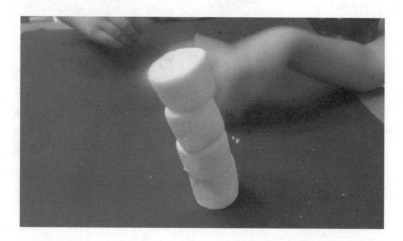

The Science Behind It

We live in a world where communication is key. Cell phone towers and radio towers are just part of our landscape now. Towers need to be strong enough to support the antennas, but also strong enough to handle a dynamic wind load. Most cell towers are built in the same way as your Marshmallow Tower.

Metal crosspieces are bolted together at the end to create the same shapes you built. The bolted together metal pieces create trusses. Trusses are strong because they redirect and share the weight load. Another great advantage to trusses is that they let wind blow through them. Since the wind blows through, they can be lighter and still add tremendous strength. Designing and building towers is an engineering skill that will continue to be needed for years to come.

Age-Appropriate Engineering

You want all ages of young engineers to feel success. For the youngest set, just having them create a tower that stands and holds a tennis ball is good. With elementary students, you might want them to hold a heavier weight. But you still want to let every team succeed, so having multiple winners is fine. For middle schoolers, you can still reward every team for making a Marshmallow Tower that holds a certain weight. At this age, you might want them to create a scale drawing of their Marshmallow Tower. This will teach the basics of engineered drawings. Drawing a flat picture of a three-dimensional tower isn't easy. For high schoolers, you could add the engineered drawings. They also should have the math background to calculate the forces in each toothpick. In high school and middle school, you may want to have a contest after they have held the desired weight. Keep adding weight till each one breaks. They will love watching them crash. As all kids know, building is fun, but so is destroying.

Dynamic wind testing is a fact when buildings are built now. Adding the fan to test the structure is one of the same tests that engineers do. They build small-scale models and put them in a wind tunnel to test them.

Pasta Bridge

Create a fun bridge out of pasta and then break it.

Engineering Challenge

Build a bridge using only pasta and glue. The bridge must be big enough for a toy car to drive across and drive under. Everybody starts with the same amount of materials. After the bridge passes the toy car driving inspection, you can add weight until it breaks, if you want. You can also allow the groups to make repairs as you add weight to correct any weak spots.

From the Junk Drawer:

- ☐ Nonstick cookie sheet or science lab table
- ☐ Linguine (long, flat noodles), at least 30 pieces per group
- ☐ Toy cars
- ☐ Marker
- ☐ Scissors or nail clippers
- ☐ Hot glue gun and glue sticks
- ☐ Small cup and coins or weights to test your bridge (optional)

Encourage the budding engineers to be creative. Shown below is just one way to do it. Read several instructions ahead if you build this style. Hot glue dries very quickly. As soon as you put it down, you want to put your pasta in it. If it dries, let it cool, pop the hot glue off with your fingernails, and try again.

Step 1: Build the bridge on a smooth, hard surface that the hot glue won't stick to. Science lab tables, granite countertops, and nonstick cookie sheets will work. Lay 12 to 15 pieces of linguine side by side. The ones you lay down for the deck of your bridge should be flat and straight— linguine noodles can be warped and curved out of the box. Any warped pasta can be used later for the smaller pieces you are going to break.

Step 2: Make sure the toy car will fit on your deck with a little extra room on each side. Add or remove noodles as needed from your deck.

Step 3: Lay a noodle across the deck and use the marker to mark the width of the deck. You might want to mark the width a little long, so you can trim it later.

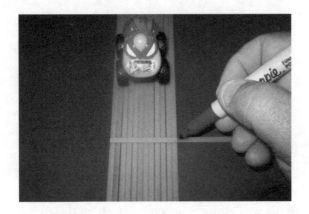

Step 4: The easiest way to get the noodles to the correct size is the two-handed snap. Grab each side very close to the mark and snap. The noodles also will cut with sharp scissors or nail clippers. You will need three noodles cut to the deck size, one each for the ends and the middle.

Step 5: Lay a bead of hot glue across one end of the deck about 2 inches or so in from the end. This will be the underside of the deck.

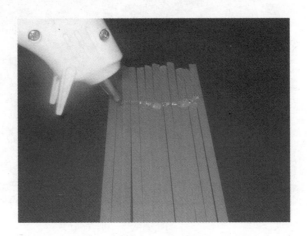

Step 6: Immediately lay one of your crosspieces down in that bead. You can use a piece of pasta to push it down into the glue. The glue will be hot for about 15 seconds.

Step 7: You can use nail clippers or scissors to trim these crosspieces flush with the edge of your deck.

Step 8: Use a pair of scissors to trim the ends of your deck square. You might want to do this over a trash can to help with cleanup. This step is not required, but it does make your final bridge look better.

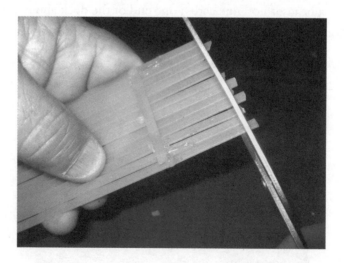

Step 9: Now you need to measure the height for your legs. Use a marker to mark a noodle a little higher than the car that needs to drive underneath. After marking, you will need four pieces that length for two sets of legs. You can use the two-handed snap or scissors to create these and any of the small pieces you need in the steps to follow.

Step 10: Lay out two legs slightly smaller than the width of the bridge deck.

Step 11: Create a diagonal brace from corner to corner. You will need four noodles cut to this length. Remember, it is OK to go a little long since you can trim them later.

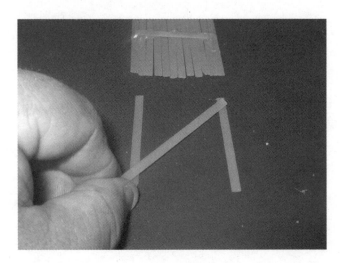

Step 12: Put a spot of hot glue on opposite corners of the legs for the cross brace.

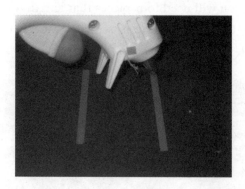

Step 13: Immediately put your cross brace on. Make sure the legs stay parallel in both directions. You should end with an *N*-shaped piece, as shown.

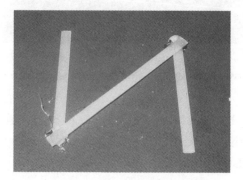

Step 14: Once cooled, turn the *N* over and put a spot of hot glue in the opposite corners to repeat step 13.

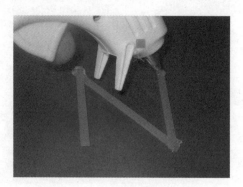

Step 15: Immediately place another cross brace in the two glue spots. Make sure the legs are parallel and the *X* in the middle is even.

Step 16: Measure and create four top and bottom cross braces. Use hot glue to attach these braces as well.

Step 17: Put a cross brace across the bottom to complete your leg assembly. Your final leg assembly should be a square with an *X* in the middle.

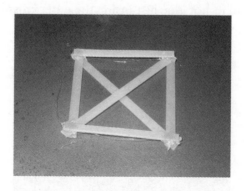

Step 18: Lay out your other two upright legs to create another leg assembly of the same dimensions.

Step 19: Repeat steps 10 through 18 to create another leg assembly.

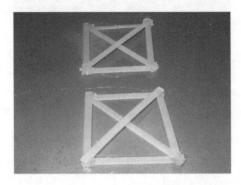

Step 20: Use scissors or a nail clipper to trim any excess pasta off the corners. It doesn't have to be perfect, and be careful not to cut off too much.

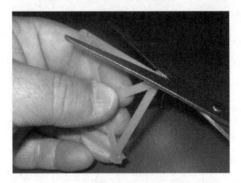

Step 21: Lay a bead of hot glue just inside the outer cross brace under your bridge deck.

Step 22: Immediately stand one leg assembly up in the glue bead. Make sure the leg assembly is perpendicular to the bridge deck. Repeat at the other end for the other leg assembly.

Step 23: Lay the bridge down on its side to add some more bracing.

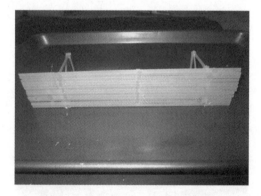

Step 24: Mark a spot 2 inches in from one leg assembly. Repeat this for the other leg.

Step 25: Put a spot of hot glue on this mark and another on the bottom of the leg on that side.

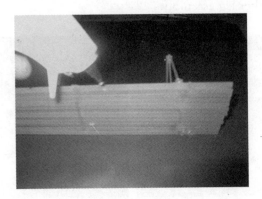

Step 26: Immediately place a full noodle on these two glue spots. One end of the noodle must be at the bottom of the leg, as shown.

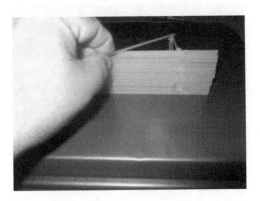

Step 27: Repeat for a leg brace on the other side.

Step 28: Check all four glue spots to make sure there is good adhesion. Add more glue if any of these joints are loose.

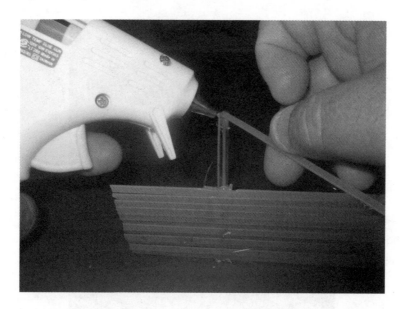

Step 29: You are going to glue where these two diagonal cross braces overlap. Lift one noodle slightly and put a spot of glue between them.

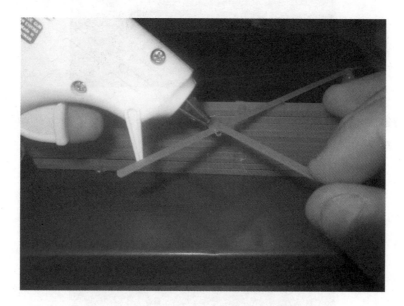

Step 30: Repeat steps 24 through 29 for the other side.

Step 31: You can stand your bridge up now. Check to make sure all of your glue spots are tight. Add more glue if needed.

Step 32: For a clean look, cut off the part of the noodles above the point where they overlap. Bridges need to be functional, but they should also look good.

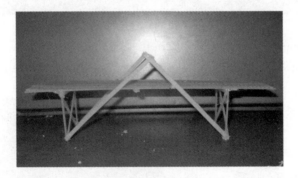

Step 33: Now it is time to test your bridge. Make sure your test car can go across the bridge deck.

Step 34: Make sure that your test car fits under the bridge.

Step 35: Now you get to test it for weight. In a classroom setting, you probably have weights you can add. In a home setting, you have to get more creative. Find a small plastic cup that will fit between your supports. You don't have to test it for weight if you want to keep it as a decoration.

Step 36: Slowly add coins to the cup. Add them gently—don't drop them with a jolt. The bridge may come crashing down at any point.

Step 37: You might even fill up your cup. You can quit there and call yourself a winner if you want.

Step 38: If the full cup didn't break your bridge, inspect the bridge for weak spots.

Step 39: You can repair a weak spot if you choose. Flip the bridge over and add glue where the bridge appears to be breaking.

Step 40: Add noodle pieces to help shore up the weak spots.

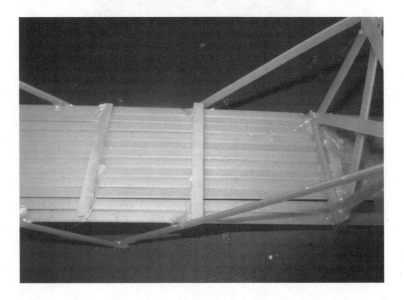

Step 41: Put the weight back on. Find more weights to add if your goal is to break it. If not, go show off your bridge to your parents and friends.

The Science Behind It

Bridges are all about strength and functionality. You need to have a bridge deck that is wide enough and strong enough to support the desired traffic. The bridge also needs to span the river or roadway underneath it. The bridge you built is called a beam bridge. A simple beam crosses between the two supports.

The supports need to be strong enough to support the bridge deck, as well as the car, truck, or foot traffic on top of it. The cross braces are important because they add strength without adding a lot of material. Look at the bridges in your area and you will notice some of the same design features you used. You can also research bridge design in books.

Bridges also serve a design feature for many cities. The Golden Gate Bridge is beautiful and among the most well-known architecture features in the world. Many big cities have similar bridges that add to the beauty of the city.

Age-Appropriate Engineering

This is a project best suited for middle school students and older. Advanced elementary students could probably do it, but might need help with the hot glue. The bridges can be built with school glue if you have time to let it dry between steps, probably overnight. If you use school glue, it is completely safe for elementary kids.

For middle school and high school students, hot glue should be fine as long as they are careful. They can add some math by doing a strength-to-weight ratio. This ratio would be the breaking weight divided by the weight of the bridge itself. They can critique their bridge and others for beauty and unique design features. They should also critique their own bridge to decide how to make their next bridge stronger.

A great art and engineering tie-in is to research the different types of bridges. They can research how the designs help to make the bridges stronger. They can find examples of each type of bridge on the Internet.

Penny Boat

Build aluminum foil boats to see what shape works the best for the maximum cargo load.

Engineering Challenge

Build a boat that will hold the largest amount of weight. The key is experimentation and design. My students get full credit for holding at least 30 pennies. We then continue adding washers to determine a winner.

From the Junk Drawer:

☐ Paper and pencil
☐ 15-cm-by-15-cm piece of aluminum foil
☐ Clear baking dish, bucket, or other container filled with water
☐ Pennies (washers or poker chips also work)

Step 1: Brainstorm ideas for a Penny Boat. You might want to draw a sketch of your ideas on paper before starting. Most good engineering designs start with a drawing. A great way to start trying shapes is to use an existing shape to create the boat. Jar lids and round cans are a great shape to try. The picture shows a can being used. Place the can in the center of your square of foil.

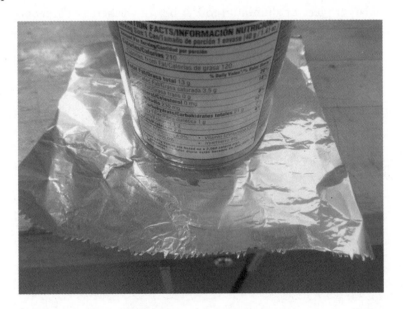

Step 2: Push the edges of the foil up around the can to create a flat bottom. The corners will extend up, but try to keep the flat sides as even as possible in terms of height. Once the foil is formed to the shape, remove the can.

Step 3: Put the foil boat in a water-filled container. Clear containers work well because you can look through the sides to see the part of the boat that is submerged. Gently add pennies to the boat. Dropping the pennies adds extra force and will sink it quicker. You want to scatter the pennies out evenly across the bottom. Poker chips are also a great choice because they are plastic and don't corrode, but they are larger so you may need to start with a larger piece of aluminum foil. A box of washers is a great classroom investment for identical weights that can be used many times a year.

Step 4: Periodically, look through the side of the clear bowl to see how much of the boat is below the water line.

Step 5: Keep adding pennies slowly, until the boat sinks. Take the pennies out, dry them off, and count them, subtracting one to get the weight required to sink the boat.

Step 6: Try a different shape. A flatter jar lid is shown here. Press the foil up around the edge of the lid, trying to keep the sides about equal height. You might want to try a smaller round container. A softball is a great way to get a round-bottomed boat if you want to try that.

Step 7: Add pennies to your new shape.

Step 8: Remember to look through the side of the container periodically to see how much of the boat is submerged. Keep adding until it sinks. Count the pennies and subtract one to get the weight required to sink it.

Step 9: A large, flat design is a great shape to test. A small box or block of wood is a great assist for making very sharp corners. Set the box on the sheet of foil about ¼ inch from the edge.

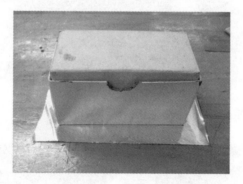

Step 10: Fold the foil up along one edge of the box.

Step 11: Turn the box 90 degrees and push the edge tightly against the side as shown, just like you are wrapping a present.

Step 12: Fold that side up to create a nice, sharp corner. Corners are the places the boat will leak, so make sure they are sealed tight.

Step 13: Repeat along each side and at each corner until you have created a large, flat boat.

Step 14: Put the boat in the water-filled container.

Step 15: Slowly add pennies one at a time. Allow at least five seconds between adding pennies. They must be very lightly laid in the boat. You also want to spread the pennies out as much as possible.

Step 16: Even with the boat almost completely submerged, you can slowly add more. Keep adding until it sinks.

Step 17: Remember to look through the side of the container to see how much of the boat is submerged. This is especially important for older students if they are doing the math with this engineering project.

Step 18: Once it sinks, count the pennies, subtract one, dry them off, and try to get more the next time.

The Science Behind It

All objects float because of density. Density is mass divided by volume. A helium-filled balloon has very little mass and a large volume, so it has a low density. The density of a helium-filled balloon is less than the density of air around it, so the balloon floats up. Boats float because they are hollow. Making a boat hollow allows the volume to be increased while the mass stays constant, so the density goes down. Large ships are made of steel, but they are hollow.

An object floats in water when the overall density of the object is equal to the density of water. The density of water is one gram per cubic centimeter. The total mass of the pennies and the boat divided by the volume of the submerged part is equal to the density of water. As you add pennies, the mass increases. The volume below the water also increases, but the density stays equal to water's density.

Even when the boat is almost completely submerged, you can still usually add a few more pennies. That is because the water will cling to the sides of the boat, which adds a little surface tension to make it hold more. If you look carefully, you can even see the sides of the boat slightly below the surface of the water because of this surface tension effect.

Once water starts entering the boat, it will sink. The slower it comes in, the longer it will take to sink. The *Titanic* took several hours to sink after water started leaking in. Modern boats have compartments below the water line that can be made airtight to help prevent sinking. Some boats, like bass fishing boats, fill the inside of the hull with foam and will never sink. Ship design is all about density.

Age-Appropriate Engineering

For the preschoolers and early elementary, just getting the boats waterproof and floating may present a challenge. But the little ones will really enjoy it. At that age, explaining density and trying different objects in water is probably enough. Try paper clips, wood blocks, and other materials.

For upper elementary and middle school students, it is time to add some math. Use a balance to get the mass of the boat and pennies and teach them how to calculate volume. In addition to their boat, they can also calculate densities of several different objects to predict flotation. You could also repeat the Penny Boat with a thicker liquid, like salt water or even corn syrup, if you feel like getting messy. Thicker liquids allow you to put more pennies in.

For high schoolers, the concept of buoyancy should be added. The weight acting down is equal to the buoyant force acting up. You can even add graphing skills. You need to know the mass of each penny, the mass of the empty boat, and the volume of the empty boat. Estimate the volume of the part of the boat that is under the water. The total mass divided by the submerged volume is equal to the density of water. You can graph mass versus submerged volume for the boats as you add pennies. The slope of the graph will be equal to the density of water. You can also repeat the Penny Boat with salt water. Salt water has a higher density, so you can put more pennies in the boat. Density is taught in most science courses, so this lab contest is fun in multiple areas.

Egg Catch

A twist on the classic egg drop challenge. In this one, you will build a device to catch a free-falling egg.

Engineering Challenge

Build a device to catch an egg that is dropped from a certain height. Supplies are limited by the instructor so that all teams have an equal starting point. Each team will have one egg to drop. Every team that succeeds from the first height will move on to a higher height.

Egg drop contests have been a classroom and competition staple for years. The problem is a really good device might be crushed, so is only good for one use. The Egg Catch is a twist in that nothing is attached to the egg and the winner is the device that can perform the task multiple times. You can put a limit on size or weight if you choose for a classroom setting. My rules only limit the overall height to 15 inches, but the judge can make other rules.

For a fun option, you can also allow the students to bring in one additional item for each group. Limit the size to something that fits in a quart-size storage bag. Future engineers then get to look at everything around them to find potential things to help. My classroom uses this option because it gives me a chance to discuss the science behind the engineering before contest day. Of course, you then get to discuss the science after the contest also.

From the Junk Drawer:

This list can be set by the instructor. My class rules are that all paper and cardboard products come from the recycling bin. Tape, straws, and string will be new. Plastic or paper cups (if allowed) must be used and rinsed out. Here's a sample list:

□ Cardboard box (maximum dimensions are suggested 15 inches by 15 inches by 15 inches)
□ 15 sheets of copy paper
□ Eggs
□ 15 straws with flexible ends
□ 15 feet of string
□ 15 inches of masking tape
□ 4 plastic or paper cups (any size allowed)
□ Scissors or serrated knife

As with all of the Engineering Challenges, the following is just one way to do it. Just balling the paper up and putting it in the box will probably allow the egg to survive.

Step 1: Stand a straw up in one corner of the box. Use two small pieces of tape to hold it in place. If you are using flex straws, you will probably want the flexible part down.

Step 2: Repeat step 1 for all four corners of the box.

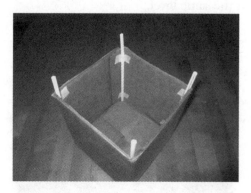

Step 3: With scissors, cut an approximately 1-inch slit in the end of a fifth straw (away from the flexible end).

Step 4: The slit allows the end of the straw to become smaller. Slide the slit end into a straw already standing in a corner of your box. The flexible end should be up.

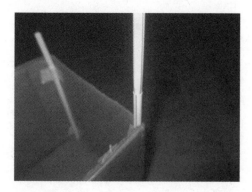

Step 5: Repeat steps 3 and 4 for all four corners. Push the straws down until they are about at the same level.

Step 6: Fold the flexible ends over as far as possible.

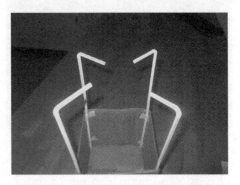

Step 7: Tear the paper into strips. You can use scissors, but tearing it is more fun.

Step 8: Wrinkle the strips up and drop them into the box. This will provide cushioning for the egg.

Step 9: Cut the bottom out of a large plastic or foam cup. You might need a knife to start the cut if your scissors don't have a sharp point.

Step 10: Wrap a piece of tape around the bottom of the cup on the outside.

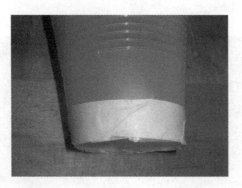

Step 11: Use scissors to cut a slit down the side of the cup till you reach the tape at the bottom of the cup. Repeat for the other side and then repeat again at a quarter turn until you have four equal parts. The tape at the bottom of the cup should keep it together.

Step 12: Add a small piece of tape to the middle of each of the four pieces at the top of the cup.

Step 13: Wrap the tape over and attach it to the bent end of the straws. You might want to wrap a piece of tape around the straw and tape juncture to make it more secure. Repeat for all four straws.

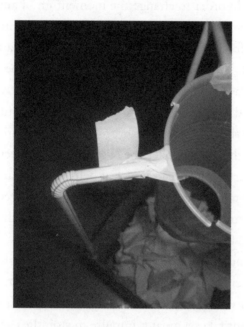

Step 14: You are now ready to drop eggs. Hit the cup and the eggs will be safe. The cup helps funnel the eggs into the waiting softness of the paper.

The Science Behind It

All moving objects have momentum. Momentum is the product of mass and velocity (or speed). In order to change the momentum of any object, you need to apply a force to stop it. And the force acts over a time interval. Engineers call the product of force and time an impulse, and it takes an impulse to change momentum. The final momentum of the egg will be zero in every case. A larger momentum requires a larger impulse to stop it.

Force multiplied by time is equal to change in momentum. The change in momentum will be the same for the egg from the first height for every group. If you can increase the time it takes the egg to stop, you decrease the force on the egg and it survives. Airbags and seat belts in your car are designed to increase the time it takes your body to stop. Trapping a soccer ball is the same concept. Increased time equals decreased force on your body or the soccer ball. Your Egg Catch device uses the same principle.

The mass of your egg is constant and the same for all groups. As the egg falls from greater heights, it will accelerate for a longer distance so it will impact with greater velocity. Greater velocity means greater momentum. So each increased height takes a greater impulse to stop the egg. The key to a good Egg Catch device is to take the longest time possible to stop the egg. More time means less force.

Age-Appropriate Engineering

For preschoolers, you might want to only drop the egg from half a meter the first time—you want all the kids to have success. Just putting all your supplies in the box will probably save the egg from this height.

For elementary age, encourage them to experiment. You can even catch water balloons to show the same concept prior to building their Egg Catch device. Many have played soccer, so trapping a soccer ball also works to reinforce the same topic. Start low enough so every egg survives the first drop. You can even adjust the height if you see a group with a weak design. They will never know if you don't give a height first. You need to break eggs at every level to let them enjoy that part. It's best to do the drops outside, if possible.

For middle school students, expect them to try to bend the rules. That is OK. Engineering is about pushing the boundaries. Allow them some freedom to interpret the rules. You want them thinking. Depending on the math level of your students, you can calculate the speed of the egg using conservation of energy. Potential energy at the top equals kinetic energy at the bottom. If both equations have been taught, you can easily solve for speed just as it hits the Egg Catch device. Mass the egg on a balance, multiply the mass by the speed and you have momentum, so that you know the impulse needed to stop the egg. Measuring the time it takes for the egg to stop in the device is virtually impossible without advanced science lab equipment. But the device that works at the greatest height has the greatest time to stop.

For high school students, they should be able to do the math. You may need to use a piece of string with a weight on it to give you a guide to hitting the device, since the heights for this age may get pretty tall. You may need a ladder or the side of a set of bleachers to allow you to go higher.

Candy Mobile

Build a whimsical mobile using candy.

Engineering Challenge

Build a mobile using candy. The complexity of this challenge depends heavily on the age of the students. A mobile uses rods and hanging weights and is a popular feature in little children's rooms. But who wouldn't want a candy mobile in their house? A simple mobile is fine for the younger set, but as they get older, more complexity needs to be required. The secret to mobiles is torque. Kids will learn about torque and when they are done, they can eat the evidence. This engineering activity is best done with at least one partner to help you hold crosspieces as you get them to balance.

From the Junk Drawer:

Option A (for elementary, middle school, and high school-age engineers)
☐ String or thread
☐ Bamboo skewers, rulers, or wooden dowels
☐ Tape
☐ Wrapped candy

Option B (for preschool and young elementary-age engineers)

☐ 3 clothes hangers

☐ Tape

☐ 4 pieces of wrapped candy

Option A (for elementary, middle school, and high school-age engineers)

Step 1: Tie a small loop in the end of a piece of string or thread. The loop needs to be big enough to fit over whatever you are using as the crosspieces. You will need to do this several times and may need to make more as you build your mobile. Some will be for hanging the candy and some will be for hanging the crosspieces.

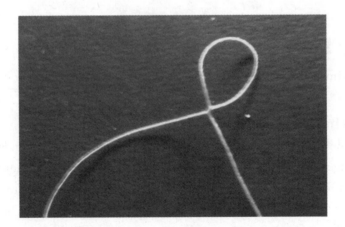

Step 2: If you are using thread or very tiny string, a great way to make the loop is to tie the string around a pen or pencil. You will also need some pieces of string that have loops at both ends to hang the crosspieces from.

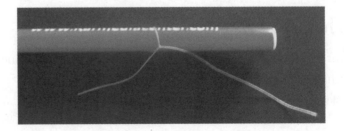

Step 3: Tape a piece of candy to the other end of the string. Repeat this for all of the candies you are going to use. Of course, you can add more if you want to get bigger later.

Step 4: Tie a piece of string around the middle of one of the crosspieces. This will be the top crosspiece of your Candy Mobile.

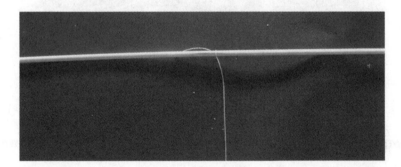

Step 5: Use tape to hang the other end of the string from the edge of a tabletop. In a classroom, you could use ring stands and lab equipment to hang the top crosspiece.

Step 6: Tie a piece of candy to either end of another crosspiece about the same distance from each end. Tie a piece of string to the center and create a loop at the top. Now the fun begins: balance the top crosspiece by hanging the crosspiece with two candies on one end and one piece of candy on the other end. You may need an extra set of hands to do this. Remember, you can slide the string loops to make it balance. This will take time and practice. You can keep adding levels if you want. It takes patience to get several levels.

Option B (for preschool and young elementary-age engineers)

Step 7: Tape a piece of candy to the end of a hanger. Repeat for a second hanger.

Step 8: Tape another piece to the other end of the second hanger. Keep the distance from each end the same.

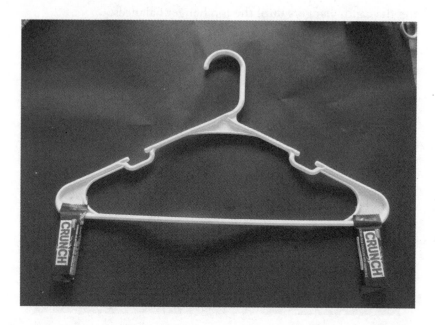

Step 9: Hang the third hanger from the edge of a tabletop using string and tape. Tie string to the top and loop it around the hanger so the hanger is free to move.

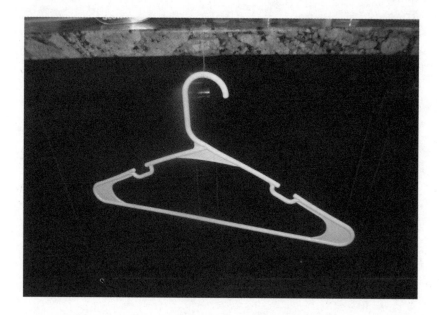

Step 10: Hang both candy hangers from opposite ends of the top hanger. You may have to provide some adult help to hold it steady as the students hang the candy hangers until the top hanger balances.

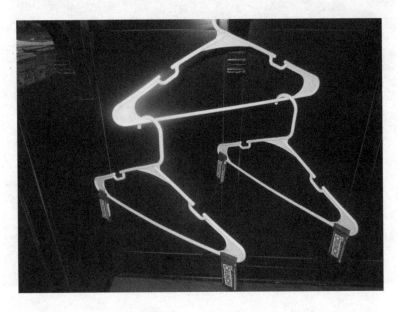

Step 11: Give one of the bottom hangers a gentle push and watch it move. Since you used string to hang the top hanger, it can spin all the way around.

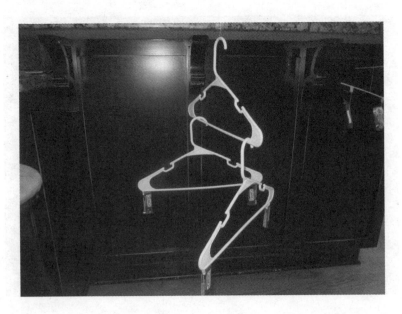

The Science Behind It

Mobiles are fun toys, and they can teach us a lot about torque. Torque is a force that causes objects to rotate, or at least try to rotate. Torque is force times the lever arm. The lever arm is the distance away from the pivot point. If the torques on both sides of the pivot point are equal, the object will not rotate. For your mobile, that means each crosspiece will remain horizontal.

The candies supply a downward force equal to the weight of the candies. So when the torques on each side are equal, the object balances. You can even balance unequal candies if you adjust the length of your lever arm. The string loops made it easy to do this. Slide the string until each crosspiece balances.

The upper crosspieces are balanced by the torques created by the suspended crosspieces and candy. You could construct crazy and complicated mobiles if you want. The nice thing about the mobiles is they also can move with the wind. They will spin and twist, but should stay balanced as long as the strings and candies don't shift. An artist who used this concept was Alexander Calder. His amazing mobiles were a combination of engineering and art. You just never know where engineering might take you.

Age-Appropriate Engineering

Option B for preschoolers allows them to see balanced torques and it is easy for little fingers. They could be introduced to the concept of torque and are probably old enough to understand balance.

For elementary age students, the concept of torque and balancing is within their grasp. They can also be introduced to the fact that torque is force times lever arm. A great way to do this is with a pencil, ruler, and coins. Balance a ruler on a non-rolling pencil and keep the balance point in the same place as you add coins. Place one coin on one side of the balance point. Stack two coins up and place on the other side of the balance point. Slide the two coins until the pencil balances gain. You have equal torques on both sides, even though you have unequal forces. The torque concept is the science behind seesaws.

For middle and high school students, they should be able to handle the concepts above easily and do Option A. In my high school classroom, they are required to mass all of the objects and do the accompanying math for at least two different crosspieces. After it is built, the teacher tells them which cross-pieces to do the equations for. They are also required to have unequal forces on crosspieces.

A great art and engineering tie-in for middle and high school students is to have them research Calder and kinetic mobiles.

SOS—Save Our Socks

Experiment, design, and build a device to keep a washing machine from eating your socks.

Engineering Challenge

Help around the house by creating a device to keep your socks from disappearing. The device must be durable, heat resistant, and not dissolve in water. It also must allow the socks to get clean.

The sky's the limit in choices here. One way is shown, but creativity is encouraged. Remember, engineering is part science and part art. My high school students always enjoy this engineering project as much as anything we do. The instructions are purposely kept very vague. The testing process is as important as the design process for this challenge. My students are surprising in their choices of materials. The testing part starts with step 3. All SOS devices must be thoroughly checked before going in the washing machine and dryer. Any device has to pass all the steps of the testing process to be OK.

If you are asking students or homeschoolers to solve this dilemma, don't discount creative (and often lazy) ways to solve the problem. We want engineers to be creative and sometimes the simplest way is best. In the past, my students have simply connected matched socks with a safety pin or binder clip. One student simply used plastic zip ties to solve the issue. It worked until he started cutting holes in his socks when he removed the zip ties. Any method that works should be rewarded.

Simple should be rewarded if it works. A Ukranian-born teacher friend of mine loved to tell a story of the Russian space program's ingenuity. NASA spent a ton of money to develop a pen that would work in microgravity. The Russians used crayons to write in space—a simple solution, and it got the job done.

From the Junk Drawer:

☐ Any material that they want to try
☐ Blow dryer
☐ Marbles, a clean rock, or any weight
   to hold device underwater

☐ Bucket of water
☐ Broom handle or paint stirrer

Suggested Supply List:

☐ Wide-mouthed plastic drink bottle
☐ Scissors
☐ Socks

☐ Oven mitts
☐ Washing machine
☐ Dryer

Step 1: Here is one simple, creative solution to the challenge: a wide-mouthed plastic drink bottle, such as those for Gatorade. The wide mouth allows you to get socks in and out, and the bottle holds up to heat and water. Test to make sure that you can actually take socks in and out of your SOS device.

Step 2: Use the sharp point of a scissors to "drill" through the side of the bottle. The holes need to be big enough to allow water through, but small enough that the socks stay inside. You can also use an awl or an ice pick with adult help. Drill seven or eight holes.

Step 3: Test for heat resistance first. Hold a blow dryer about 6 inches from your SOS device. The device will get hot, so have oven mitts nearby. Also, make sure you are testing it on a heat-resistant surface, like a concrete driveway or granite countertop. My students test their device outside, just

to be safe. The judge needs to disqualify any devices that are obviously flammable. The blow dryer needs to be aimed at the device for 10 minutes. In a dryer, the clothes (and your SOS device) keep tumbling, so the heat doesn't stay directly applied to the device for longer than that. My students have never told me of a problem with any SOS device that passed the 10-minute test. Any device that melts in 10 minutes won't work. Remember, the device is hot, so let it cool down.

Step 4: Steps 4, 5, and 6 are best done outside for easy cleanup. Add a weight to your bottle to keep the device submerged. In a classroom setting, anything that is clean and sinks will work. Avoid objects that will rust.

Step 5: Fill a large, clean bucket or bowl with clean water. Submerge the device in the bucket. Now comes the fun part. Use the broom handle (or paint stirrer) to vigorously stir the object for 10 minutes. A team approach is best for this, since after a minute or two, you will get tired of stirring. It is OK, and actually advisable, to hit the device as you stir. You are simulating the thrashing your SOS device will take in the washing machine.

Step 6: After 10 minutes, allow the water to settle. Look carefully in the water for pieces that have broken off. Broken pieces of almost anything in a washing machine could permanently damage the machine. Broken pieces send you back to the planning stage to revise your device.

Now move the bucket to a safe inside area, like a garage. Let the SOS device sit submerged in the water overnight. Inspect the water and SOS device thoroughly the next morning. You are looking for anything dissolved in the water, or anything different about your device.

Step 7: Make sure you have permission from your parents before you try a successful device in the washing machine or dryer. You probably want to try it by itself in the dryer for a limited amount of time first to make sure it will work. Then, once you know the device is safe, add your socks and try again.

The Science Behind It

Lost socks have been the scourge of humankind since we started wearing them. Periodically, socks just disappear. There are several likely causes and your SOS device can solve a few of these. The first case is the missing sock never made it into the washing machine. Odd socks are in your couch, the backseat of your parent's car, or hiding in your bedroom. Your SOS device won't save these, but you might know it earlier.

The other culprits will be fixed by your SOS device. Socks are light and small, so they can actually disappear. In a top-loading washing machine, socks can float over the top of the inside drum. They get trapped between the spinning inside drum and the outside tub. Repeated spinning turns them into fuzz that goes out with the water. An odd sock can also get jammed under the center agitator and chewed up eventually. Your SOS device should prevent both of these calamities. Switching to a front-load washing machine has cut down on the orphan socks around our house. (You can also skip this engineering activity altogether and celebrate diversity with mismatched socks. But designing a device to save socks is a fun engineering challenge.)

The testing process here is probably more of the engineering than creating your SOS. You are testing for heat resistance with the blow dryer. You are testing for durability as you stir the device in water. And finally, you are testing for whether anything on the device will dissolve in water.

Engineers build models of devices they want to test all the time. These models are called prototypes. A prototype allows the testing and design of an actual product and not just an idea on paper. For very large objects like airplanes, they will create a small scale model first. Remember, engineering is about the design, building, and improving the device. Testing is one way to improve the design.

Age-Appropriate Engineering

This activity probably only works well with students in middle school and above. Make sure the testing is thorough before you use a washing machine. An occasional lost sock is better than a broken washing machine.

3

Waves

Light and sound are two different waves we use all the time. Waves carry energy. We can use that energy to light a room or speak to our grandparents. The use of waves in engineering has grown immensely in our connected world. Using waves to send information may be the fastest growing form of engineering right now.

Let's use waves to transfer some energy.

Talk Talk

Expand on the classic can-and-string phone.

Engineering Challenge

Create an old fashioned two-cup phone and then experiment with different receivers and materials for the string. Also find out how to let even more people listen in on your conversation.

From the Junk Drawer:

☐ Plastic or Styrofoam cups
☐ Soup can (only use cans you have opened with a safety can opener)
☐ Pushpins or hammer and nail

☐ String
☐ Paper clips (optional)
☐ Safety can opener

As always, the material list can be modified by what you have on hand. You may also want to try materials not on the list. Experimentation is the key to engineering.

Step 1: Use a thumbtack or pushpin to create a hole in the bottom of two cups. If using soup cans, you might need a hammer and a nail to create the hole.

Step 2: You will need to wiggle the pushpin around to make the hole bigger. The thread or string will have to slip through the holes. Teachers or group leaders with younger children may want to do the first two steps ahead of time to avoid the use of the pins.

Step 3: Cut a long piece of string. The longer the better, but the length might be a function of room size. In a classroom setting, I usually allow the kids to test the Talk Talk in the hallway. One half the length of a football field will work with the right string. Slide the string through the hole.

Step 4: Tie a giant knot in the string on the open side of the cup. The knot must be larger than the hole. An even easier option is to tie the string around a paper clip. The clip will pull tight against the inside of the cup and not slide through the hole. Repeat for the other cup.

Step 5: With a friend, pull the string tight by stretching the cups as far as the string will let you go, but don't pull too hard. One person should talk into the cup while the other holds the cup to his or her ear. The "ear" person can say out loud what he or she heard. The string phone works like a charm. Switch the talker and the ear person and have a conversation.

Step 6: Create a second string phone by repeating steps 1 through 5. In a group setting, just pair partners up. Wrap the string of the second phone around the string from the first phone. Slide one cup under the original string and then pull the cup over the top of the original string.

Step 7: Now all four partners pull their string tight. One person talks and the other three listen. Take turns being the talker.

Step 8: With a larger group, repeat steps 6 and 7 and create a conference call (optional).

The Science Behind It

All sound is caused by vibration, whether your vibrating vocal chords cause the air to vibrate, or whether your tabletop vibrates when you drum on it. Sound is a mechanical wave which means it has to have a material to travel through. When you talk into the cup, the vibrations of the air from your voice cause the cup to vibrate. The vibrating cup causes the string to vibrate, and the vibrating string causes the other cup to vibrate. The vibrating ear cup causes the air inside it to vibrate, which causes your eardrum to vibrate. The string acts as the material that transmits the vibrations.

Some materials transmit sound faster and better than others. Try different types of cups and cans to try to create the best sounds. Different types of strings, metal wire, and rubber bands will transmit sound better. Experimentation is the key.

Age-Appropriate Engineering

For preschool to young elementary students, just creating the string phone is enough. Teaching them about sound, vibrations, and waves is the key. For upper elementary to middle school-age students, teaching all of the above is important, but you might want to add in how the human ear works. You can also explain that some waves, like light, don't need a material to move in and can travel through empty space.

For high school students, all of the above are important. You can also add an in-depth study of waves. For really advanced high school students, you can use function generators and oscilloscopes to mathematically examine the waves created. I create these string phones every year, even with my college-bound seniors in advanced placement physics, as an introduction to waves. They absolutely love it. For 15 minutes or so, they behave just like six-year-olds and it is fun to watch. It is also a great easy lab to stress the importance of experimentation by trying different materials.

Sound Explosion

Create a mini amplifier from a paper towel tube, and then make it boom.

Engineering Challenge

Build a mechanical amplifier and find the best way to create a big boom. Two different ways are shown, one using earbuds and one using only the phone. You can use a phone app to measure the boom when you are done.

From the Junk Drawer:

☐ Paper towel tube   ☐ Empty milk jugs
☐ Marker   ☐ Tape or hot glue
☐ Sharp knife   ☐ iPod or cell phone
☐ Scissors (optional)   ☐ Second phone with sound level
☐ Plastic cups   application

Step 1: Stand your cell phone (or iPod) up on the center of the paper towel tube. Trace around the bottom of the cell phone with the marker, as shown.

Step 2: Get parental help or permission to use a sharp knife. Cut out the shape created by the marker in the previous step. For younger children, have an adult start the hole by cutting a small slit and let the kids finish the cuts with scissors. Don't cut it all for them; they need to get the feeling they did it themselves.

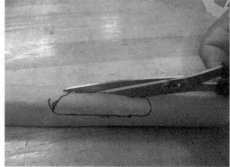

Step 3: Test fit your phone into the hole you just cut. Depending on the weight of the phone and the strength of the paper towel tube, you may have to lay the phone down. Just make sure the speaker is pointing up when you slide it into the tube.

Step 4: Hold the end of the paper towel tube against the side of the plastic cup. Trace around the edge with the marker. Repeat for both cups. Milk jugs, rinsed out used drink cups, and orange juice cartons also could be used. Milk jugs will need to have the top cut off with a sharp knife. With younger children, you can start the cut and let them finish with scissors.

Step 5: Cut out the circle using a sharp knife. As previously stated, an adult can start the cut and have younger children finish the cut with scissors. Test the fit of the tube in the hole and trim the hole if needed.

Step 6: Experiment and test your Sound Explosion device now. Slide the paper towel tube into both cups. Start up some music on your phone, and then slide it into the top slot and listen to the sound explode out of the cups.

Step 7: Another experiment is to test what angle works best to create the loudest sound. Does standing the cups up make it louder?

Step 8: Experiment with how far the paper towel tube must slide into the cup for best sound. Once you find the best distance into the tube, seal the tube to the cups using tape or hot glue.

Step 9: You can also use another phone and find a sound level decibel meter app. There are many free versions out there. Of course, you may need parental permission or have them download it for you.

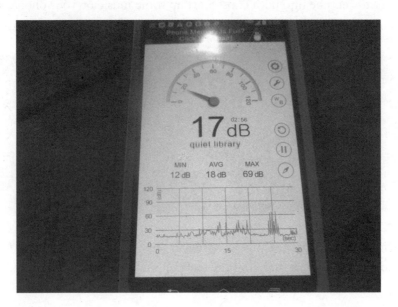

Step 10: Try it again, experimenting with different speaker cones. Try milk jugs, paper cups, Styrofoam cups, potato chip cans, and anything else you can imagine.

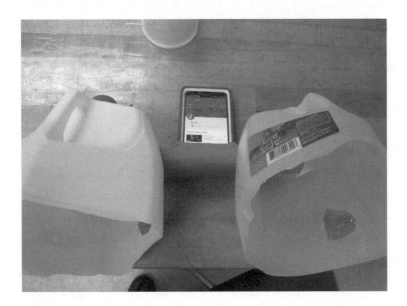

The Science Behind It

The Sound Explosion amplifier is a mechanical amplifier. The Sound Explosion amplifier "traps" the sound waves and directs them out of the front of the cups. The cups and the tube also create a larger sounding board by vibrating at the same frequency as the music being played, so that you end up with a larger vibrating area which creates a larger sound. With the addition of directing the trapped sound waves being sent toward you, you get a Sound Explosion.

Most sound amplifiers electrically amplify the sound. An electric amplifier takes the sound wave and electrically increases the amplitude. A traditional volume control allows the speaker cone to vibrate with a larger displacement. Larger displacement equals louder sound. Many speaker boxes are designed to use the same process you used to mechanically amplify the sound, in addition to electrically amplifying the sound. A good speaker and amplifier give you both mechanical and electronic amplification. Your mechanical amplifier may put you on the path to becoming an audio engineer.

Age-Appropriate Engineering

This is a great project for all ages. Younger children probably don't have their own cell phones, but one adult's cell phone would work to test each Sound Explosion device. The best part is they can take their Sound Explosion devices home to their parents to show off what they made. Most cell phones are similar in size, but the parents (or kids) could trim the phone hole for any phone. Parents love to see their kids are learning. Little ones will love the sound level application on the phone. But be prepared, they are going to yell to try to create the loudest sound.

For middle and high school students, they will take them home and many actually use them. You can also introduce the decibel loudness scale. For high school students and advanced middle school students, you can even go into the math to help teach them a logarithmic scale, since the decibel scale is a logarithmic scale. High school students will also become louder than kindergarten students as they try to create the loudest sound possible on the sound level application.

Mirror, Mirror on the Wall

Use mirrors and a laser pointer to hit the target.

Engineering Challenge

Use mirrors to direct a laser beam to hit a target. Set up a laser pointer on a flat surface. Create a target somewhere else in the room, or even another room if you do this at home. Using a set number of mirrors, direct the laser beam to hit the target. The challenge is how to hold the mirrors at the correct angles as you hone in on the target. The complexity can be easily adapted for every level of student.

From the Junk Drawer:

☐ Laser pointer (use a very small, low power red laser pointer to prevent eye damage)

☐ Several mirrors (number depends on complexity of challenge)

☐ Paper target

□ Tape or rubber bands

□ Various objects to support the mirrors, like magazines, textbooks, pillows, backpacks, playing cards, etc.

□ Meter sticks, paper, pencil, and protractors for older students

□ Hairspray or talcum powder (optional)

The three options shown here are for the various levels of students. Sometimes students don't fit in a certain age bracket because of aptitude and how complicated the lead engineer wants to make the challenge. For example, if you just want to teach the law of reflection to high school students and don't want to devote a lot of time, the first simplest option may be the best. Also, if you have an advanced elementary age student who likes a good challenge, the high school level challenge may be the best. The key thing is to learn some skills and have fun.

Regardless of age or level, read all the options for helpful hints and messy options. Teachers should probably demo the messy option, but students love to see it. We used chalk dust for years, so if you still have a blackboard, just bang two chalk erasers together. Dry erase dust never works in my classroom, but you could try.

Option A: For Elementary-Age Students

Step 1: Place the laser pointer on a very steady surface. A dining room table or lab table is a great option. You are probably going to need to elevate the laser pointer 1 inch or so to clear any frames on the mirrors. A book or a block of wood could provide a great base. Use a small piece of tape or rubber band to secure it. You don't want it to move for the entire engineering activity.

Step 2: Stand a target up to one side of the laser pointer. Use books or a block of wood to hold it up. You could use a toy as a target, but a bull's-eye is fun and easy to draw. You could even have the little ones draw them. The center of the bull's-eye needs to be at the same height as the laser pointer.

Step 3: Stand a mirror up to be perfectly straight upright. Use a piece of tape to keep it upright. You need to be able to move the mirror and its support, so use a small food can, block of wood, empty aluminum can, etc.

Step 4: Turn the laser pointer on. Never shine a laser pointer in your eye or anyone else's eye. You may want to use a small piece of tape to hold the button down if you have a limited number of hands. If you have enough people, just have one press the button when it is needed.

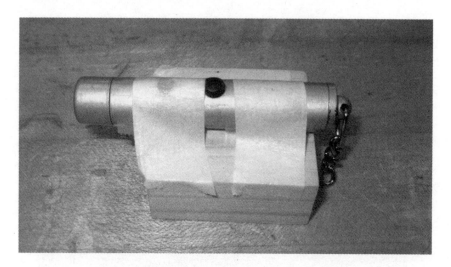

Step 5: An easy way to adjust the height of your laser is to use playing cards. Use as many as needed to get the pointer to the correct height. It must hit the mirror when turned on. You can also use playing cards to adjust the height of your target if needed.

Step 6: Place the mirror and support at the other end of the table. Slightly angle the laser pointer and the target till they create a long, skinny *V*.

Step 7: Slowly spin the mirror and support until the light hits the target.

Step 8: Take a look at how close you are to the target's bull's-eye. Adding playing cards to your target is a great and easy way to make the height right.

Option B: For Middle School and Upper Elementary Students

Step 9: For higher level students at this age, put the target at the end of the table opposite from the pointer. Add another mirror on the same end as the pointer. Twist both mirrors until the light makes a *Z* and hits the target.

Step 10 (Optional): Laser light only shows up when it has something to reflect off of. You can see it on the target and on the mirror, but you can't see it in between. This is because air molecules are too small to reflect the light. If you spray a little hairspray between the mirror and laser, you will see the laser beam because the hairspray particles are big enough to reflect light. A very, very light squeeze of talcum powder will also do the same thing. Just a little will show it to you; if you add more, you have to clean more. There is no photo of this step since it doesn't show up on film well.

Option C: For High School and Advanced Middle School Students

Place the target at a different height on the other side of the room and ask them to hit the target. Be prepared to see all sorts of crazy engineering to hold the mirrors steady and at the right angle. You could even put the target on another floor if you do it in your house and then direct the laser beam up the stairs.

The Science Behind It

Mirrors work by the law of reflection. The law of reflection states that the incident angle (incoming angle) to the mirror is equal to the reflected angle (outgoing angle) when compared to a normal line. The normal line is a perpendicular line at any point on a surface. For flat mirrors like those used for this challenge, the normal lines are all perpendicular to the surface. The light from the laser is going to bounce off at the exact same angle as it hits. So if the light comes in at 45 degrees, it leaves at 45 degrees. By moving your mirrors to the correct angle, you can hit the target.

Curved mirrors, like in a funhouse or makeup compact, still use this same principle, but the back of the mirror is curved so the normal lines aren't all perpendicular. This causes the image in the mirror to look funny. The law of reflection always works for mirrors.

The other engineering aspect that makes this a fun activity is laser light. Laser light is of a single frequency (color). All of the photons of laser light are also perfectly lined up, so laser light travels in a very straight line. Normal white light is a combination of colors that don't all line up, so white light scatters all over the place. Laser light is like first graders lined up going down the hall to lunch. White light is like first graders on a playground during free time.

Age-Appropriate Engineering

For elementary age students, a single mirror on a flat table is probably enough to introduce them to the topic. They can be introduced to angles and reflection. You can also see the same concept by bouncing a ball back and forth between two people, as long as you don't spin the ball.

For middle school students, you can increase the number of mirrors on a flat surface. You can also push the envelope with putting the target at a different height. They will have to use crazy engineering skills to hit the target by positioning the mirrors at just the right heights and angles. You can also have them take measurements after the fact and draw a scale picture. Make sure to draw the mirrors at the correct angle. This is probably done most easily for the tabletop version, but can be done for the multi-height laser and target if the students are good at math. After they draw the picture, they can use a protractor to measure the angles.

For high school students, it depends on the course. For an introductory course, the single-mirror, all-flat setup is enough to teach the basics of the law of reflection. For an advanced course, the sky's the limit. For my advanced placement level students, I don't turn the laser on. They have to make measurements and decide where and at what angle to place the mirrors. They have to set everything up before they turn the laser on. Afterward, they are allowed to reposition the mirrors to hit the target while the laser is on. After making a drawing, they measure the angles using a protractor to verify the law of reflection.

This is an incredibly versatile engineering activity that will help the students understand a little more about light and mirrors. As always, all children are different and what you are trying to teach them is different. Feel free to use any of the options to best push your little engineer.

Musical Mystery

Create a homemade musical instrument and play a tune. Use smartphone apps to see your musical wave.

Engineering Challenge

Create a completely homemade musical instrument and play a musical song. The instrument can be percussion, stringed, or a wind style. There are numerous ways to do this.

From the Junk Drawer:

Any material could work; the material list below is for the featured instrument

☐ ½- or ¾-inch PVC pipe scrap (at least 3 feet long)

☐ PVC cutter or hacksaw and adult help

☐ Ruler

☐ Scrap plastic lid from recycling bin

☐ Permanent marker

☐ Scissors

☐ Hot glue gun and hot glue

☐ Smartphone with sound app downloaded (optional)

This challenge has many solutions. Xylophones and drums are easy to make. Shoe box guitars are also easy. Fill eight glasses with different amounts of water and you can create an eight-note musical scale. You can play them by blowing across each glass or even slapping the top with a flip flop.

The following instructions are to create a pentatonic pan flute. A pentatonic scale only uses five notes to create a scale. It is easier for smaller hands. You can make an eight-note scale pan flute with straws using similar instructions.

Step 1: Cut a length of scrap pipe about 8 inches long. A PVC cutter makes this easy, but you will need adult help to cut the pipe. It can also be cut with a hacksaw. Make the cut as straight as possible.

Step 2: Cut another piece about 1 inch shorter.

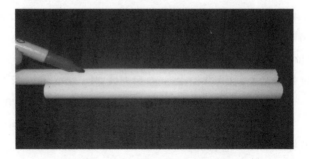

Step 3: Cut three more pieces, each one about 1 inch shorter than the previous. You will end up with five pieces, measuring 8, 7, 6, 5, and 4 inches.

Step 4: Stand one tube up on the scrap lid you rescued from the recycling bin. Use the marker to trace around the bottom of the tube. Repeat five times.

Step 5: Use a good pair of scissors to cut the circles out. Kitchen scissors are a good choice if you have some available.

Step 6: Lay the five circles out on an easy-to-clean surface, like granite or tile.

Step 7: While holding one tube in your hand, apply a bead of hot glue around one end of the tube.

Step 8: Immediately press the hot glue bead onto one of the plastic circles. Repeat steps 7 and 8 for all five tubes.

Step 9: Use a ruler to even up all the open ends of the tubes.

Step 10: Place a piece of tape across the five tubes. Individualize it with colored tape, like fancy duct tape or masking tape you can color on.

Step 11: Turn your pan flute over.

Step 12: Press the tape down.

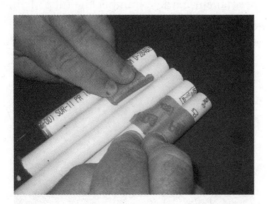

Step 13: Press another piece of tape on this side and wrap it around to hold the pan flute together securely.

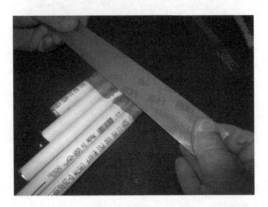

Step 14: Repeat the previous steps to add another piece of tape around the pan flute at a lower point. This will help make the pan flute very sturdy.

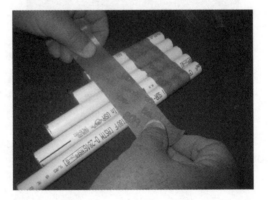

Step 15: With a permanent marker, number the tubes 1 through 5, with 1 being the longest tube.

Step 16: Blow across the top of one tube to create sound. Vary how hard you blow and the angle you blow at. Your ear will tell you what the best combination is. You are now ready to play a song. A simple one to play is "Mary Had a Little Lamb." Blow across the tubes one at a time in the following order: 3 2 1 2 3 3 3 2 2 2 3 4 4. Practice the song, then go show it off.

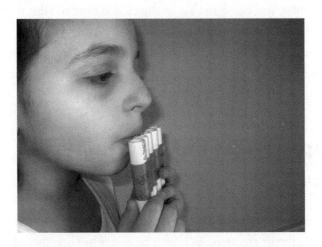

Step 17 (Optional): There are many free applications for a smartphone that will tell you what note you are playing. Analyze each tube to see what note it plays. You can take the flute apart and trim each tube until you get exactly the note you want. Always err on the long side as you cut the tubes. You can always cut it shorter, but you can't add length. This takes a ton of patience, but if you are into music, it is worth it.

The Science Behind It

All sound is caused by vibrations. The medium that vibrates can be a solid, a string, or air. Vibrating solids are the key to a xylophone. The size of each part is different, so it vibrates at a different frequency. Different frequencies are different sounds. Wind chimes work the same as a xylophone. You can actually play music on a wind chime. Put pleasing frequencies together and you have a song.

Vibrating strings are the keys to guitars, harps, and pianos. The thickness of the string and the tightness of the string determine the frequencies. Just bite one end of a new rubber band and pluck it as you pull it tighter and you will hear the different frequencies. Playing multiple frequencies at the same time is a chord. Strumming a guitar when different length strings are held at the same time is the easiest way to see that. Your homemade musical instrument can probably only play one frequency at a time, but it is a great way to start.

Vibrating air columns are the key to brass and woodwind instruments, and your voice. The pan flute shown is an example of this type. As you blow across the top of the tube, you cause the air in the closed pipe to vibrate. Different length pipes create different frequencies.

Air is essential for almost all instruments, since sound won't travel in a vacuum. There may be no sound in outer space. But there will be plenty of sound in your space with your Musical Mystery instrument.

Age-Appropriate Engineering

Children like noise. After all, sound is just noise to people that don't like it. Every age will enjoy this engineering activity.

For the youngest children, simply creating the sound and understanding notes are just different frequencies might be enough. They should also be able to grasp that vibrations create sounds.

For elementary age children, sound can be studied more deeply. They should also be able to make instruments that create sounds. Playing simple songs should be possible at that age. They can also understand that sound does not travel in space.

For middle and high school students, the instruments will get more complex. They can probably use a smartphone and apps to tune their musical instrument. Vibrations are included in almost every science course for these ages.

Secret Monitor

Turn an old flat-screen monitor into a super-secret monitor.

Engineering Challenge

Take apart an old flat screen monitor and create a working monitor screen that is only visible through your secret filter. Only you can see the image and you will learn about polarized light at the same time.

From the Junk Drawer:

- ☐ Old flat screen computer monitor
- ☐ Tools (most will need a flat and a Phillips screwdriver)
- ☐ Scissors
- ☐ Cup for storing hardware
- ☐ Alcohol (or other cleaner) and rag
- ☐ Old sunglasses or 3-D glasses from the movie theater
- ☐ Marker
- ☐ Calculator

Step 1: You will need an old working flat screen monitor. Disconnect the computer cable and the power cord. These can be removed directly from the monitor and left connected on the other end.

Step 2: The next few steps are to remove the plastic case around the screen. This usually requires a screwdriver, but some just pop off. First remove any stand that holds the monitor up. This monitor had a button that would release the stand, but all monitors are different.

Step 3: Remove any screws that are on the outside of the plastic case using your screwdriver. There may not be any on some monitors, but if they are there, remove them.

Step 4: Keep all the hardware you remove in a cup to keep it together.

Step 5: You are going to remove the front plastic frame next. Most are held on with plastic tabs. You need to pop those plastic tabs off in one spot first. Some are easy enough to do with your fingers, but most require a flat screwdriver. Slide the flat end of the screwdriver under the frame and gently lift. You might need to move it to the right or the left to find the tabs. Try to do it without breaking the face frame, but if it breaks, it can be taped back in place at the end.

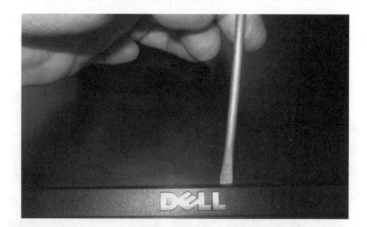

Step 6: Once you pop the first tab, you can probably pop the rest with your fingers. Slowly work around the face frame trying not to pull too hard.

Step 7: Be careful around the buttons on the front of the frame. You want to leave those buttons connected.

Step 8: Fold the plastic face frame up out of the way, but leave the strip that connects the buttons intact. It should fold easily to the top to get out of your way for the next few steps.

Step 9: Most monitors have an inside metal frame. You need to remove it also. You need to be able to get to the edge of the flat glass screen. Remove any screws around the edge and put them in the cup from earlier.

Step 10: Once all the screws are out the metal piece should separate from the back piece. Most monitors have two metal rectangles that sandwich the screen.

Step 11: If the edge of the front glass screen is exposed, proceed to the next step. You might need to pry the metal frame off if it is attached to the glass screen. Use a screwdriver to slide in one of the slots and very gently pry the metal away from the screen.

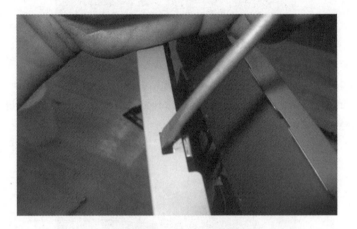

Step 12: Use extreme caution with this step. Use the flat edge of a pair of scissors to get under the top layer of plastic on the flat screen. Always use the blade moving away from your body with gentle pressure only. The corners may break off and that is OK. Our goal is to eventually be able to pull off the largest piece possible.

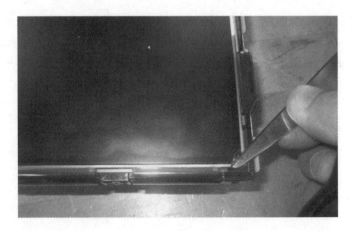

Step 13: Slowly move the scissors back and forth to create a larger area to get your fingers under. Once you can get your fingers under the corner, proceed to the next step.

Step 14: Slowly pry up the flexible plastic piece on the front. It is important to take your time to pull off the largest piece possible.

Step 15: If the screen is curled, lay it out flat under some type of weights, like blocks of wood or soup cans.

Step 16: Clean the glass monitor off. The monitor will have residue from the glue holding the plastic filter on it. Alcohol and a rag will work. There are also many removers (like Goof Off) that work even better if you have them around already.

Step 17: Now reassemble the frame back on the flat screen monitor. You are going to reverse the steps you did to take it apart. Your monitor may be different than the one shown. Snap the inner frame back on the clean glass monitor.

Step 18: Replace any screws as you put it back together.

Step 19: Putting the screen back into the plastic outside case may take a screwdriver to pry up the plastic case as you slide it in. Take your time and it is possible.

Step 20: Snap the front frame back onto the plastic back frame. Start in one corner and work your way around the monitor. Put the stand back on the monitor and attach the power cord and the monitor cable.

Step 21: Clean off the back of the plastic film you pulled off the monitor. Use the same cleaner you used for the glass monitor screen.

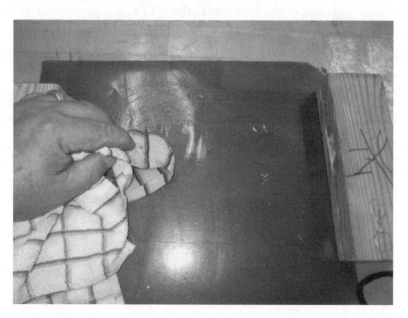

Step 22: Turn on the computer and it will open to the desktop. Look at the screen. What do you see? Now look at the screen through the flexible plastic layer you removed earlier. Turn the flexible plastic layer over and you may see the colors invert, although not always. Move the flexible layer different distances away from the screen. Find the distance where it allows you to see the screen the clearest. If it is pretty clear at all distances, you can try the optional steps following. If it becomes really fuzzy when moved away from the screen, doing the optional steps won't help much.

Steps to Create Super-Secret Monitor Sunglasses

Step 23: For this step, you will need a pair of old sunglasses. You can also use 3-D movie glasses, if you have some. The 3-D movie glasses can be bought very cheaply on the Internet. Do not take them from an actual movie theater, unless they are single-use, disposable glasses. Old, cheap sunglasses can also work. If you look through 3-D movie glasses, each lens will create a different color. You will still see the image on the screen, but the different colors are produced because the lenses are polarized at different angles.

Step 24: Lay the glasses on top of the flexible layer and trace the outline of the eyepieces.

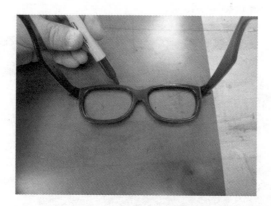

Step 25: Use scissors to cut along the inside of the tracing marks you made.

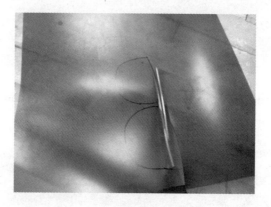

Step 26: Pop the lens out of your old glasses.

Step 27: Push the new lenses you just cut into the frames. You may have to trim them to fit correctly. Use tape to hold them in place if you are struggling to get it to work.

Step 28: Look through the glasses at the monitor. Move the glasses out of your vision and watch what happens.

Using a Calculator to See a Cool Effect

Step 29: Take the piece of film you have left and look at your calculator. Rotate it until the calculator screen is completely dark.

Step 30: Now rotate the screen until the numbers come back. You have just seen polarized light at work.

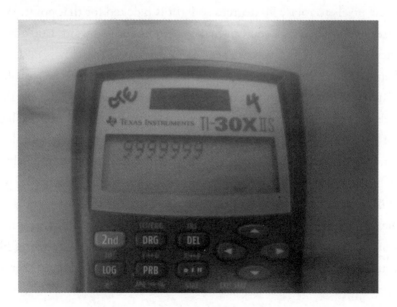

The Science Behind It

Most monitor and calculator screens work because of polarized light. Light is a transverse wave, which means the wave parts move back and forth while the energy moves. Normally, this back-and-forth vibration is at many different angles. Polarized film only allows one direction of vibration to get through.

Imagine this to get a better picture of polarized light. Put a rope through a picket fence. Picket fences have straight up and down slats. If you wiggle the rope straight up and straight down, the wave goes through unchanged. But if you wiggle the rope at another angle, part of the rope hits the picket slats so the wave is changed. If you wiggle it completely sideways, nothing would get through the slats.

The calculator display (steps 29 and 30) is the simplest way to explain what goes on with your monitor. The screen consists of two polarized sheets of film, like you peeled off the computer screen. The two polarized sheets are turned 90 degrees from each other. Sandwiched between the two is a layer of liquid crystal and tiny, nearly invisible electrical wires. Normally, two polarized sheets that are 90 degrees to each other block all light. But since the liquid crystal causes the wave to rotate 90 degrees, the screen you see is clear. When electricity is applied to individual points (pixels) in the liquid crystal, the liquid crystal causes the pixels to rotate 90 degrees so light is blocked for that point. With the correct points blocked, you can make any number you want. Look carefully at a calculator display and you can see the individual dots.

Your computer monitor does the same thing, but the pixels are smaller and more numerous. Color monitors use red, green, and blue filters on very tiny subpixels to make up a pixel. By controlling the voltage to each subpixel, the color of each subpixel varies. By varying those three colors, you get a color display. And there are thousands more pixels in a monitor. You might be able to see the individual pixels in an old computer monitor with a magnifying glass, but probably not with the newest monitors.

The calculator display is easier to understand, but the computer monitor is more fun to watch. Since you are looking through one of the polarizing filters, only you see the picture and nobody else. You have created a Secret Monitor.

Age-Appropriate Engineering

This is probably the only engineering project that is strictly for the older students. The concept of polarization is taught along with waves. This is a great way to show it to upper-middle and high school students. You can show it off to the younger crowd and they will be amazed, but understanding polarized lights and filters is probably beyond their brain development.

$g = 10 \text{ m/sec}^2$

$E = \frac{1}{2} mv^2$

potential energy

$s = \frac{d}{t}$

torque

$W = mg$

$F = ma$

$\frac{force}{area}$

$pressure = \frac{force}{area}$

$f = \frac{1}{T}$

Glossary

catapult: device to launch projectiles that uses an elastic material to store energy

elastic potential energy: energy possessed by a material that stretches and bounces back to its original length

energy: the ability to do work, can be potential (stored) or kinetic (in action)

force: any push or pull

frequency: number of vibrations per second, usually measured in Hertz (Hz)

gravitational potential energy: energy an object has because of its position in a gravitational field, depends upon weight and height

impulse: the product of force times time, can change the momentum of an object

kinetic energy: energy of motion, related to mass and speed

laser light: single frequency light that will travel in a very straight line

law of reflection: states that the input angle and the output angle will be equal when measured from a normal line

moment of inertia: a number that tells you how easy an object will roll or spin.

momentum: a measurement of motion that is equal to mass times speed

normal force: a perpendicular force out of a surface that balances out the force that an object pushes into the surface

normal line: a line perpendicular to a surface

polarization: allowing only one direction of light wave to travel

pressure: force per unit area

projectile: any object that has been launched without a means of power after being launched

radius: the measurement from the center point of a circle to the edge

stability: how well a structure avoids being knocked over

torque: a force that causes objects to rotate; depends upon force and distance from the pivot point

trajectory: curved path of a projectile after being launched

truss: a framework of struts used to support objects

waves: a means of transferring energy

weight: the pull of gravity on an object, acts toward the center of the Earth